D1572132

Alaska's
Homegrown Governor

A Biography of William A. Egan
by Elizabeth A. Tower

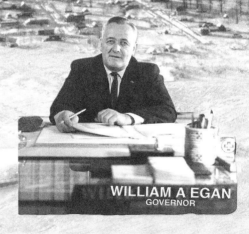

WILLIAM A EGAN
GOVERNOR

PO Box 221974 Anchorage, Alaska 99522-1974

ISBN 1-888125-99-3

Library of Congress Catalog Card Number: 2003105754

DEDICATION

To Valdez

The fertile soil where seeds of Alaska statehood took root and produced a generation of political leaders, like William A Egan, who were instrumental in creating a new state and guiding it through its infancy.

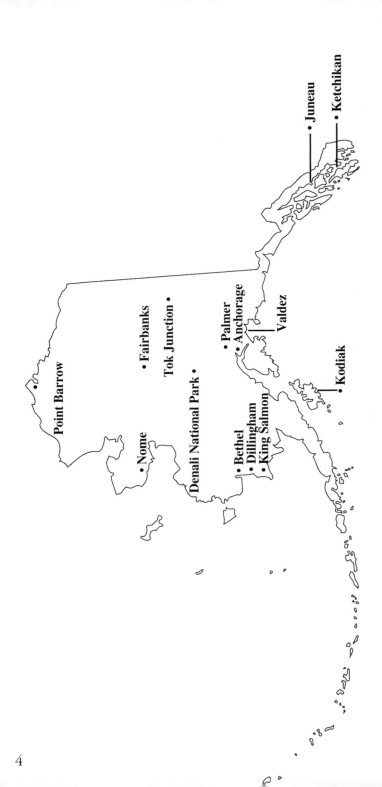

Point Barrow

Fairbanks
Tok Junction
Denali National Park

Nome

Palmer
Anchorage
Valdez

Bethel
Dillingham
King Salmon

Kodiak

Juneau
Ketchikan

CONTENTS

INTRODUCTION

W hen planning Alaska's Constitutional Convention in 1955, the territorial legislators were aware of a parallel to America's fight for independence more than 150 years before. They decided to have 55 delegates because a like number framed the United States Constitution. After these delegates wrote Alaska's Constitution, they instigated a revolution of their own by advocating the Alaska-Tennessee Plan and sending an elected congressional delegation to Washington D.C. to demand statehood for Alaska.

The plan succeeded and Alaska achieved statehood in 1959. William A. Egan, with a solid legislative background and experience framing the constitution, was an appropriate choice to guide the new state through its crucial early years. Alaskans, like the American colonists, resented years of taxation without representation and economic strangulation by powerful non-Alaskan resource exploiters. They wanted to be led by a man whom they recognized as a true Alaskan they could trust. Egan, born and schooled in small-town Valdez, filled the bill. His Valdez roots may have been Egan's greatest asset because Valdez was neutral ground in the new state, torn by geographic factionalism. Egan was not allied with Anchorage, Juneau or Fairbanks. Above all, he wanted Alaska to function as a united state.

Alaska, like the United States, had a fascinating group of founding brothers. The relationships among Ernest Gruening, E.L."Bob" Bartlett, and Egan is an interesting study in itself. Although he died prior to statehood, Anthony J. Dimond should be included as a founding brother because of his influence on both Bartlett and Egan

In this book, I have concentrated on Egan's early life, attempting to point out factors that helped prepare him to be Alaska's first governor. In the early twentieth century, Valdez produced a generation of political and business leaders that included, in addition to Egan, George Sullivan, who served as Anchorage mayor for 15 years, guiding Alaska's largest city through unification with the Greater Anchorage Area Borough in 1976; John Dimond, one of the first State Supreme Court justices; Dan Cuddy, president of the First National Bank of Alaska; and John Kelsey, Valdez businessman and former chairman of the board of directors of the Permanent Fund Corporation.

Egan faced many challenges during his three terms as governor, including organization of the state executive and judicial branches, state land selection, establishment of a state ferry system, reconstruction after a Richter 9.2 earthquake, foreign fishery incursions, settlement of Native land claims, development of a taxing structure for the oil industry, and construction of the trans-Alaska Pipeline. His governorship years will be described briefly with no attempt to critique his policies and performance. In future years such analyses will, undoubtedly, be made by students of government who can look back on Alaska's early statehood years with the perspective of time.

FAMILY

O̲n Easter afternoon in 1921, the Egan family waited on the Valdez city dock for the return of the five-man crew working at a mine on Shoup Glacier south of Valdez. Six-year-old Billy turned to his mother and said, "My father isn't coming home." Soon four avalanche survivors confirmed the boy's premonition. The contractor, 54-year-old William Edward Egan, died in a massive snow slide early that morning.

Shoup Glacier where Bill Egan's father, William Edward Egan, was killed in an avalanche on Easter morning in 1921.—Photo courtesy of Geoffrey Bleakley.

The April 2, 1921 issue of the *Valdez Miner* carried the details:

Wm. Egan was killed and three companions were buried Sunday morning, March 17, by a huge snowslide which swept down the mountainside behind the property of the Valdez Mining company, about seven miles back from the waterfront, on Shoup Glacier. Mr. Egan, in company with Gus Kring, Fred Johnson, Fred Erickson and Ed Stone, was engaged in shoveling out the tram cable which is needed to haul supplies from the lower camp to the upper. The slide, which came without warning, buried the four men, Gus Kring being saved by the slide breaking across the canyon about 300 feet above him. Mr.

Kring, who was the sole witness of the disaster, states that he was engaged in shoveling when he heard the roar of the approaching avalanche, and when he looked saw the crest of the snow wave strike Mr. Egan and Mr. Stone, who were several hundred feet above him. It had already buried Johnson and Erickson farther up the mountain side. Mr. Kring hastened to the spot where he had last seen Messrs. Egan and Stone and started digging them out, being joined later by

William Edward Egan was killed when his son Bill was six years old.—Photo courtesy of Gerald Bowkett.

Johnson and Erickson who had worked their way out of the loosely packed snow over them. ... Mr. Stone was found first, a few feet below where the slide engulfed him. He was nearly dead from suffocation and the pressure of the pack. After he was revived, the work of searching for Mr. Egan was taken up, and his body was found a few yards above the spot where Stone was rescued. He

was dead when uncovered, as first aid administered failed
to indicate any signs of life. Death apparently was in-
stantaneous and painless as there were no indications of
a struggle. ... Funeral services were held in St. Francis
Xavier's church of this city. ... The remains were laid to
rest in the Valdez Cemetery at 10 o'clock this morning.
... As a man Mr. Egan was among our best citizens. He
made friends and held them wherever he was engaged in
work and Valdez has lost heavily by his untimely death.

Young Billy never had an opportunity to see much of his
muscular father who was often away from home doing
contract work at the hardrock gold and copper mines in
the mountains surrounding Valdez. Since mining was at
a low ebb in the Valdez area and there was strong com-
petition for contract work, William Egan had felt it necessary to get an early start on his work at the Shoup
Glacier mine even though he had observed on a recent
hunting trip that the weather was unseasonably warm
and the snow unstable. Egan was a devoted family man
who, according to daughter, Alice Egan Horton, "used to
spoil us kids when he came home." Clinton, the oldest
Egan son, described his father as a man of medium height,
"wiry like a mountain goat", who would take the older
boys ptarmigan hunting. The older boys had started
working with their father on some of his contract jobs
during the summer.

The Egans, like many mining families had moved west
and eventually to Alaska seeking new opportunities in
the mines. William Edward Egan, originally from New-
foundland, moved first to Nebraska and then to Montana, where he worked in the copper mines. While in
Montana he met and married Cora Allen. By 1902, when
the Egans moved to Douglas, Alaska, to work in the
Treadwell mine, they had three children, Clinton, Emmet and Ethel. While in Douglas, five-year-old Clinton

fell from a dock and broke his back. He was in the hospital in a plaster cast for eight months and continued to have a hunchback deformity throughout his long life. The following year, after Clinton recovered from his injury, the family moved to Ellamar on Valdez Arm, where William Edward found work in a copper mine. They moved on to nearby Landlocked Bay where a third son, Alaska, was born in 1904. In 1906, the family moved to Valdez, which was thriving in the anticipation of becom-

Egan family photograph, taken around 1917, shows, left to right, Cora Allen Egan holding baby Francis, Alice, Ethel, Bill and Alaska.—Photo courtesy of Gerald Bowkett.

ing the port city for a railroad to the interior of Alaska and rich copper mines in the Wrangell Mountains. A second Egan daughter, Alice, joined the family early in 1907. By the time William Allen Egan was born on October 8, 1914, the boom in Valdez was over. Following the 1907 shootout between rival railroad construction companies in Keystone Canyon north of Valdez, Cordova was designated as the future port city for the Copper River and Northwestern Railroad and work on the Valdez right-of-way was suspended. Some of the Valdez population moved to the new town across Prince William Sound. Completion of the railroad from Cordova to Chitina in 1911 and construction of the Edgerton Cutoff between Chitina and the Richardson Highway established a transportation route to Fairbanks and the surrounding mines that competed with Valdez, which had previously been the only Prince William Sound port serving the Richardson Highway. In 1914, the selection of Seward as port city for a government railroad up the Susitna river route to Fairbanks killed any hopes that Valdez would ever get its railroad. The future looked bleak. More Valdezians moved out and re-

Young Valdez lawyer, Anthony J. Dimond, right, shown here with James Lathrop, center, and Eddie Rusher, left, was Bill Egan's godfather.—Valdez Museum AC 1996.30.11LC.

located in Seward or Anchorage, the new railroad construction town on Ship Creek. Valdez was reduced to a mere 400 residents. The editor of the weekly *Valdez Miner* tried to look on the bright side, commenting that Valdez was now reduced to fighting trim. In the midst of this depressing outlook, William Edward Egan took a step that undoubtedly contributed to the future success of his fourth son when he asked young Tony Dimond to be William Allen's godfather.

Dimond family photograph, taken around 1930, shows Marie and John Dimond, standing, and Dorthea and Ann, seated.—Rasmuson Library UAF 68-69-816.

Anthony J. Dimond, who would become Alaska's delegate to Congress from 1933 to 1945, had just returned to Valdez to practice law with Thomas J. Donohoe after spending a year as magistrate in Chisana, a remote gold rush camp in the Wrangell Mountains. Egan and Dimond both arrived in Valdez in 1906. They shared mining backgrounds and the Roman Catholic faith. Dimond was forced to give up mining after sustaining a gunshot wound in the leg. While confined to the Cordova hospital for a year with chronic osteomyelitis resulting from the injury, Dimond studied law with Donohoe, who maintained law offices in Cordova and Valdez. Dimond demonstrated his commitment to settle permanently in Valdez in February 1916 when he married Dorothea Miller, whose father had been a prominent Valdez merchant before his death. After his marriage Dimond quickly became a community leader. The Dimond's eldest daughter Marie was born later that year, as was the fifth and last Egan son Francis. The Dimonds and Egans were neighbors and Marie and her younger brother John were friends and playmates of the younger Egan children.

While practicing law with Donohoe, Dimond became active in the Democratic Party because Donohoe was Democratic national committeeman during the Wilson administration. Donohoe traveled extensively, leaving Dimond to fill in for him in his absence. In 1919, Donohoe moved to Cordova and Dimond took over the Valdez office. Although Dimond initially resisted suggestions that he run for state office, he soon became active in local politics. He was elected to the Valdez City Council in 1917, 1918 and 1919. As recipient of the largest number of votes, he was designated as mayor the last two years.

The Egans were not as active politically and socially as the Dimonds but William Edward served a term as a Valdez school director in 1909. With so many children, he had a special interest in the schools. Cora Egan, a stocky

15

woman of average height, had her hands full at home. The older Egan sons, however, were prominent members of the younger crowd. Clinton served as a page in the 1913 session of the Alaska Territorial Legislature in Juneau and Emmet was active in the Young People's Literary Society, writing articles on school affairs for the local newspaper and participating in debates. When the United States entered World War I, Emmet volunteered for the Twentieth Engineering Corps. In May 1918, he wrote his parents from Fort McDougall in California that he liked army life and wished he had enlisted earlier. By October, Emmet was in France in combat during the last campaign of the war. Bill Egan recalled his brother's return to Valdez during the winter of 1920 when the Valdez harbor froze solid.

During the summer of 1920, both Emmet and Alaska Egan worked for their father, who had a $35,000 contract to drive a big tunnel at the Alaska Gold Company mine on Shoup Glacier. When construction ceased for the winter, Emmet took a job at The Pinzon bar, which would play an important part in the subsequent life of the Egan family. The eldest Egan daughter, Ethel, left Valdez to take stenographic training in the Juneau area.

Although both Emmet and Alaska were in Valdez at the time of their father's death, they left town the following summer to work on construction of the Alaska Railroad. Life in a small, isolated town like Valdez no longer appealed to the able-bodied older Egan sons. Alaska subsequently worked for newspapers in Seward, Takotna and Fairbanks, while Emmet went to the San Francisco area to work on bridge construction. They never returned to live in Valdez or did much to contribute to the support of the family. Neither brother married and, in later years, the Valdez family was contacted to cover funeral expenses when they died without assets. Francis, the youngest brother, contributed to the family by doing odd jobs until he was old enough to follow his older brothers and leave town permanently. He returned to Valdez once in 1941 to see his mother and then served in the merchant marine during World War II. After receiving a $200 loan from his brother Bill in 1971 to cover gambling debts, he was never heard from again.

Cora Egan sued the Alaska Gold Company and received a $4,600 settlement in May 1922, but it was not sufficient to compensate for the loss of the primary breadwinner. Aside from the income that Cora was able to make taking in laundry, selling house plants, doing home nursing, renting rooms, and serving occasionally as a jail matron, support of the family became the responsibility of Clinton, known generally by his nickname, "Truck", after a well known baseball player of the time. With his deformed back, Truck could not participate in the mining and freighting activities that were still the mainstays of the Valdez economy. He found employment liquidating stock at the Valdez Mercantile Company, which attorney Warren Cuddy had taken over as receiver. After that job ended, he worked for several other Valdez stores. Billy did whatever he could to help the family and was especially proud to be able to buy his school clothes with money earned in a fish processing plant when he was ten years old.

Valdez school children and teachers in 1926: 1, John Kelsey; 2, Dan Cuddy; 3, Joe Dieringer; 4, David Cuddy; 5, John Dimond; 6, Bill Egan; 7, Roy Dieringer; and 8, Frank Egan. MB68.14.23, Anchorage Museum of History and Art.

COMMUNITY LIFE IN VALDEZ

Bill Egan rarely talked about his boyhood in Valdez, but some of his childhood friends are able to give a picture of life in that small, isolated, and depressed community during the 1920s and 1930s, and to provide some insight into the factors that contributed to the success of Egan and his contemporaries. John Kelsey, a Valdez community and state leader, summed it up in *Valdez: A Brief Oral History:*

> We had some pretty good models in our parents. ... You know Mr. Tony Dimond... he was a self-made attorney. ... The Cuddy father was a business man and then he moved to Anchorage, bought up stock in the First National Bank and eventually owned the majority of the stock and took over the bank... The Gilson family - they went on - John became president of the (Valdez) First National Bank. ... George Sullivan became deputy marshal and then mayor of Anchorage. ... Bill Egan, of course, is history. ... An interesting generation, I feel fortunate to be a part of it. I'm sure none of us ever thought that we were going to do anything different than maybe become a truck driver or longshoreman, or a fisherman—which a lot of them did. But a lot of us chose to do other things.

Cash was in short supply in Valdez. Most of the boys started working by the time they were in their early teens since there was no enforcement of child labor laws. During the summer they worked in fish canneries and stevedored on the Valdez dock. With no restrictions on driving age, they learned to drive automobiles as soon as they were available and earned money taking visitors on tours of Keystone Canyon. Egan started working for the Alaska Road Commission when he was 14, driving an old Model T dump truck and then a Model A. The *Valdez Miner* described an incident in which young Egan saved a friend from possible injury:

> Roy Dieringer had a narrow escape from serious injury Thursday evening when his arm became entangled with the shaft of the automobile he was driving. Roy and Billy Egan were taking the car to the garage, and before driving in, Roy got out to drain the water from the radiator. The engine was left idling and the clothing on Roy's arm became caught on the drive shaft which runs the pump, and wedged so tightly as to stop the motor. Quick action on the part of Billy Egan, who cut and pulled on Roy's sweater and shirt, saved him from serious injury. As it was he got off with a ruined sweater and shirt and a badly bruised hand.

During the winter, work was harder to find. Only one boat a week came in to the Valdez dock, so boys were dismissed from school to work as stevedores. Egan also had a job taking tickets and cleaning up at the Valdez Theater in the Eagle's Hall, and eventually became a projectionist. School, of course, was the primary winter activity for the Valdez children and teenagers. Bill Egan threatened to quit school so he could help support the family after his brothers, Emmet and Alaska, left town, but his brother Truck insisted that he graduate from high school.

Valdez school children had a special opportunity to observe government in action. Since Valdez was the seat of the Third Judicial Division Court, students attended court sessions as part of their school curriculum. They also met people from all over Southcentral Alaska when they came to Valdez to serve on juries or be witnesses at trials. The judges and trial lawyers became their heroes.

Third Division Court in Valdez, where school children could observe the judiciary in action until the building burned in 1940.—Russell Dow collection UAA Archives.

They watched L.V. Ray, the golden-tongued orator from Seward, and Tony Dimond, who utilized his own disability to advantage when representing injured workers.

Community activities in Valdez often included the children. On Saturday nights parents would drag the kids

Heavy snowfall in Valdez made it possible for children to build tunnels.—Russell Dow Collection UAA Archives.

along to the community dances. John Kelsey recalls that as the way he learned to dance. Otherwise the young people made their own fun. In the winter when snowfall in Valdez was heavy, George Sullivan recalls building 300-400 foot tunnels in the snow, complete with escape chutes. Bill Egan's special friends were his only classmate, George Ashby, and the Dieringer brothers. One summer Egan and Ashby organized John Kelsey and other younger boys into a platoon of "army" soldiers. Every morning the boys had to report to "Sergeant" Egan. Then they would march around town carrying wooden rifles with Egan calling cadence. Kelsey recalls that Egan seemed to enjoy this feeling of authority. The younger boys enjoyed teasing Egan and playing tricks on him because they could get a good rise out of him without having him hold a grudge. The young pranksters were especially fond of going around to target different houses, especially the school teachers'. They would plug up the chimneys to smoke people out and turn off electric fuses on porches. On one occasion John Dimond credited Egan with saving his life. As a Halloween prank, the boys stuffed wet towels in the chimney of a hall where the older crowd was having a party. When smoke filled the hall, a man ran out and chased the boys with a knife. Egan interceded in the nick of time and forced the knife from the man just as he was about to attack young Dimond.

As soon as the Richardson Highway closed for the winter, basketball games began. Egan played basketball in school and later on a town team that challenged the high school varsity. Although he was short, Egan was quick and scored well as a guard. He wrote imaginative accounts of some of these games for the local paper and probably was the author of a column entitled "Sports by the Alaskan." Egan was always interested in sports and considered himself an authority on boxing. Once, while attempting to teach John Dimond to box, he was surprised to have his tall, lanky pupil land a punch that sent him reeling through the front window.

The Egan, Dimond and Sullivan families attended the Catholic church in Valdez. George Sullivan recalls that Egan served as an alter boy in his early teens. On one occasion Egan was reprimanded for stepping out of character to extinguish the flames when a candle set the priest's robe on fire. Egan stopped attending services after the Dimond family left Valdez in 1932.

Valdez old-timers recalled that Egan was "kind of a nervous little guy" when he was growing up. Although Egan's writing ability won him the job of writing for the local paper, public speaking caused him considerable anxiety. Egan and George Ashby were the only two students in the 1932 graduating class at Valdez High School. While giving the salutatorian speech at graduation, Egan got halfway through before he got so nervous that he had to quit and leave the stage. Valedictorian Ashby continued reading Egan's speech. In later years Egan improved his public speaking by practicing in front of a mirror. Egan's

Valdez Catholic Church where Bill Egan served as an alter boy.—Russell Dow Collection UAA Archives.

shyness did not prevent him from participating in events organized by the Valdez Staghounds, a club "formed to make the dismal evenings of winter seem more pleasant." A typical Staghound party was described in the January 17, 1931, *Valdez Miner:*

> The Valdez Staghounds gave a tin can shower for Mr. and Mrs. Russell Keith at the Moose Hall last Saturday night. Games and dancing were indulged in with the radio and phonograph furnishing music for the occasion. A feature of the evening was a hockey game be-

tween James Dolan's team, consisting of himself, Harold Gillam, Dick Reed, and Billie Egan, which defeated Walter Day's crack team, George Ashby, Adolph Dieterle, Charles Swanson and Beauford Clifton, by a score of 4 to 3. Later the guests of honor opened their numerous gifts and a lunch of hot dogs, buns and coffee was served.

Marie Dimond was among the young ladies attending this Staghound function.

EARLY FLYING ADVENTURES

T he Valdez boys had an oppor-
tunity to observe the early days of bush flying in Alaska.
Valdez had one of the first air strips in Alaska even though
the surrounding mountains made it a dangerous place to

*Owen Meals with his OX-5 Eaglerock biplane in which
13-year-old Bill Egan took his first airplane ride.*—Photo
courtesy of Talkeetna Museum.

fly. Bush pilots met the incoming steamships in order to
pick up passengers and freight bound for Fairbanks and
other interior destinations. R.W. Stevens, a retired West-

ern Airline captain and aviation historian, described young Bill Egan's first flying experience:

> Owen Meals, Valdez Ford dealer and garage owner, brought the first airplane to Valdez, and had almost completed the assembly of the *Spirit of Valdez* on June 9, 1928. The OX-5 Alexander Eaglerock biplane was built with two open cockpits, one in the rear for the pilot and one up front, which could seat two passengers. Meals

Aerial view of Valdez in 1932 when Bill Egan started his flying lessons.—Russell Dow Collection UAA Archives.

> had learned to fly the previous winter at the factory in Denver. The pilot took it aloft for an initial test hop on July 11, 1928, landing an hour later to take his wife, Nancy, up as the first passenger. Billy Egan, thirteen at the time, was so young it was necessary for his mother, Cora, to sign the `waiver of responsibility' section on his ten-dollar ticket. On July 18, Jack Cook and Billy Egan became the eighth and ninth passengers, taking a twenty minute ride huddled together in the cockpit, the excitement of it all never to leave them.

Young Bill's enthusiasm for flying earned him the distinction of being aviation editor for the *Valdez Miner* even before he graduated from high school. In this capacity he wrote accounts of the comings and goings of bush pilots such as Harold Gillam and Alex Holden. On May 21, 1932, an article in the *Miner* announced the arrival in town of Frank Pollack, a pilot specializing in student instruction, "having soloed close to 50 students the previous year." Pilot Pollack gave Valdezians an "excellent exhibition of his flying ability" one Thursday morning and the following afternoon "his first Alaskan student, Billy Egan, started his flying time." Egan's flying instruction sometimes had unexpected benefits for his friends, as reported in the *Miner*, undoubtedly in Egan's own words:

> Last Sunday evening, while giving flying instruction to Bill Egan, Pilot Frank Pollack spotted a large black bear a short distance north of the dike, near the ball grounds. The fliers circled over him, giving Mr. Bruin what was probably the worst scare of his life. They then landed and sent out information to hunters that the animal was close in, after which they took off again, found the bear, and Pollack began cutting circles around bruin, who was making good time toward the hills north of town. As the plane cut across his path whatever way he turned, the bear became bewildered and did not know which way to turn. In the meantime George Ashby, E.C. Chase, Harold Starkel and Jim Dieringer started out in pursuit of the now thoroughly bewildered animal, which was being held at bay by the circling plane. Dieringer was the first to come in sight of bruin and with a shot from his trusty rifle laid the animal low. The bear was loaded on a truck and brought to town.

Even though Pollack indicated that Egan was one of his smartest students, other Valdezians didn't have as much confidence in Bill's ability. Years later Ed Lindahl, who owned the plane that Pollack was using, recalled that Pop Huddelston had taken him to task for "taking money from a kid that can't learn to fly."

After graduation Egan continued to write flying columns for the *Miner* and occasionally served as a stringer for the Associated Press, which liked to print material about the exploits of Alaskan bush pilots—especially glacier pilot

Glacier pilot Bob Reeve with the plane in which Bill Egan served as "bombadier".—Russell Dow Collection UAA Archives.

Bob Reeve, who arrived in Valdez in 1932 just as Egan was successfully completing his first solo flight. Egan impressed Reeve and soon began working for him in various capacities. Reeve delivered supplies to mines located on glaciers in the mountains around Valdez by having a passenger drop them from his circling plane. The "bombardier" had to be tied into the plane so that he would not fall through the open door when the plane was in a steep bank Of all the Valdez boys that served in this capacity with the glacier pilot, Egan earned a reputation for making the most accurate drops without breaking any of the contents. An article in the *Miner* described another type of support work that Egan performed for Reeve:

Wednesday morning, Lou Townsend and Bill Egan mushed over the Valdez Glacier to the Ramsey-Rutherford mine to ascertain and mark off the most suitable place to be used as a landing field. Townsend and Egan returned to Valdez Saturday afternoon. They report having staked off a spot in the creek bed which is over 1,600 feet in length and which, considering the altitude, will be a most ideal place in which a plane may land at this

Bob Reeve pioneered the art of landing on temporary fields at the gold mines on Valdez Glacier.—Russell Dow Collection UAA Archives.

time of year with freight and passengers. The men report a long, hard trek enroute to their destination, owing to the soft snow which made trail breaking quite difficult. They were unable to leave the regular switch-back trail as drifts and soft snow made this route extremely dangerous, so they proceeded on to the Wilson barn and cabin and made their crossing there. It is approximately nine miles from Valdez to the Wilson cabins and about three miles from there up a ten per cent grade to the mine. It

took the pair about nine hours to reach the mine bunk-
house Wednesday, but on the return trip today, they
reached Valdez in four and one-half hours. There is a
good deal of snow on the glacier, they said, and most
small crevices are filled with drifted snow.

By the time Reeve and Egan flew in to the mine the
next day, snow had already obliterated the poles mark-
ing the field.

On March 10, 1934, the *Miner* reported that Reeve would
soon start freighting supplies to the mine and that "Bill
Egan will assist Pilot Reeve on this end and will later go
to the mine where he will be employed for the summer."
An increase in the price of gold during the nationwide
depression stimulated interest in gold mining in Alaska.
Mines that had been dormant for years were being worked
again in the Valdez area. Work at the mine undoubtedly
paid better than Egan's previous summer work driving
trucks for the Alaska Road Commission and laboring with
the local Civilian Conservation Corps.

The following winter, an article in the *Miner* indicated
that Egan had qualified for the title of "mechanic" and
was accompanying Reeve on some of his flights. The
following article, probably written by Egan, provides a
good description of the flying hazards that he encoun-
tered in his youth:

> Pilot Bob Reeve with Mechanic Bill Egan and Rich-
> ard Zehnder, a passenger, set his Fairchild `51 down
> at the home airport at 2:50 p.m., Tuesday afternoon
> after a hazardous flight from Fairbanks. Reeve and
> Egan left Valdez for Fairbanks on December 1.... Af-
> ter spending two days completely overhauling the ship
> Reeve intended to make the return flight to Valdez.
> However, Monday night, December 3, Fairbanks was

visited by the first December rainstorm on record. Tuesday morning the Fairbanks field was bare of snow and the warm weather still held out. The flyers, whose ship was on skis were marooned in the interior metropolis praying for snow so that they could get off the ground. The temperature dropped a little and the next morning the field was covered with frost. Reeve immediately warmed up his ship, and by using all the

Bill Egan, right, with oldtime miner and prospector, Andy Thompson, at the Ramsey-Rutherford gold quartz hardrock mine where Egan worked in the early 1930s. —Photo courtesy of Gerald Bowkett.

skill acquired from hundreds of hours of Alaska flying conditions, forced the ship off the ground and started for his home port, Valdez. The flyers ran into a dense fog near McCarty and had to circle for some time before finding an opening south. Near Rapids the clouds were so thick and so high that they had to fly low and keep under them. At Isabella Pass clouds closed in below, behind and above the ship and the flyers were forced to ascend to an altitude of about ten thousand feet to clear them. The rest of the flight to Valdez was made at a high altitude with nothing but a blanket of clouds between the plane and the ground. Reeve also reports having trouble with his wings and controls icing up on him. The flyers reported that Fairbanks and the interior sections of Alaska have been having their share of unusual weather conditions, temperatures of from 50 to 60 above zero having been recorded there the past week. All flyers who had changed to skis in the interior section are now back on wheels and the absence of snow presents a serious problem to trappers and various other people who are in the hills.

Later that winter Egan collaborated with Reeve on another hazardous expedition that had a less fortunate outcome. Pilots Reeve and Owen Meals located a local man who was lost on the glacier but were unable to revive him. Egan and Irving Beeman, who had followed by dog sled, were left with the frozen body. They reported that bringing the body to town was a difficult job for the dog team, the snow being deep and soft, and one of the dogs giving out. The sled would catch on boulders under the snow, and it kept the men busy holding the body on the sled. John Kelsey remembers that Egan seemed to live a charmed life and is amazed that he survived because he was always the first to go out on searches and rescues missions.

When Bill Egan was not busy with other jobs, he worked at The Pinzon bar, which his brother Truck bought with a partner in 1927. The Pinzon was the social center for the men and boys of Valdez, featuring snooker, pool and billiard tables, and a card room where pan and pinochle were played, in addition to an ice cream fountain and bar. The Pinzon sold magazine and newspapers, cigars, cigarettes, candy, and Nenana ice pool tickets. (Alaskans traditionally bet on the time ice in the Nenana River will break up in the spring.) Boys and young men enjoyed fraternizing there with old-timers who had lots of stories about the gold rush days in Alaska, but women and girls were not usually welcomed. After prohibition ended in 1932, The Pinzon obtained a liquor license and Bill often served as bartender.

By 1936, Egan had sufficient income to buy a second-hand Studebaker and the following year he purchased an Aeronica C3 from W.H. Dunkle. Egan had to go to

The Pinzon bar where Bill Egan worked for his brother Clinton "Truck" Egan—Russell Dow Collection UAA Ar-

Anchorage to pick up his plane. Against all advice he was determined to fly it back to Valdez by devising an apparatus that allowed him to pump extra gas from the cockpit into the external tank while flying. He planned to land the plane on the Valdez mud flats, but heavy snow made it necessary to pancake the plane in a snow drift instead. Egan flew locally around Valdez and Prince William Sound until the Aeronica burned in a hanger fire in 1939. George Sullivan recounts an episode when Egan offered him a ride to town from his work site at a nearby mine. "We just barely got off the ground and then he began diving and barrel rolling. I straightened him out by threatening him with a fire extinguisher." Katherine

Bill Egan with the Aeronica C3 that he purchased from W.H. Dunkle. The plane was destroyed in a hangar fire in 1939.—Photo courtesy of Gerald Bowkett.

Ashby recalls that he used to fly around town and lean out of the cockpit to yell at people on the Valdez streets. However, neither his brother Truck nor his friends felt that Egan had any desire to fly commercially.

YOUNG DEMOCRAT

Bill Egan might have pursued a career in aviation had it not been for the development of an even more compelling interest in politics. During Egan's senior year in high school, his neighbor and god-father, Tony Dimond, announced his intention to run for

Anthony J. (Tony) Dimond, standing with cane, rode in the car with President Warren Harding when he visited Alaska in 1924.—Anchorage Museum of History and Art B82-46-39.

delegate to Congress. Dimond had already served two terms in the Alaska Territorial Senate in addition to being mayor of Valdez. He demonstrated his popularity with voters when he was reelected to the Territorial Senate in 1928. His fellow legislators respected his ability and energy. The Democratic primary was a three-way contest between Dimond, George Grigsby, a lawyer who had previously run unsuccessfully for delegate, and A.H. Ziegler from Ketchikan. Dimond won the Third Division easily with 82.6 percent of the vote as well as the Second and Fourth Divisions. In the 1932 general election he faced Delegate James Wickersham, who ran unopposed in the Republican primary and showed no inclination to retire although he was 75 years old. Wickersham campaigned in his usual bombastic oratorical style, attacking Dimond as a corporation lawyer who represented the Guggenheim interests in Alaska.

Dimond's campaign style impressed the editor of the Seward paper, who commented:

> If anything, Senator Dimond went far to inject into Alaska politics something of substance and clarity, totally ignoring the time-honored custom of mudslinging, so characteristic of Territorial campaigns in the past. When called upon to meet accusations and innuendo thrown out by his opponent, Senator Dimond displayed rare qualities in his aptitude in marshalling political records in lieu of personal opinions.

In a television interview many years later, Egan attested to Dimond's dignity and gentlemanly manner as compared to Wickersham, whom he considered to be "an old windbag." Dimond won the election easily with 72.3 percent of the 13,759 votes cast.

Upon arriving in Washington, D.C., in 1932, Dimond was surprised to discover the severity of the nationwide depression. Alaska actually was suffering less than the rest of the United States and the population of Alaska was even growing slightly after a long slump following World War I. Dimond approved of Franklin D. Roosevelt's relief policies and became an ardent proponent of the New Deal. Since he was Alaska's sole representative in Washington, D.C., the delegate had the dual responsibilities of serving as advocate for Alaskans when dealing with various federal agencies operating in Alaska and of interpreting New Deal programs for his constituents back home.

As a method of keeping Alaskans appraised of political happenings in Washington, Delegate Dimond regularly sent copies of the *Congressional Record* to interested parties back home. Truck Egan, who succeeded Dimond as mayor of Valdez, received the *Congressional Record* regularly. Truck's interest in politics was limited to local issues, but young Bill became Alaska's most dedicated reader of the *Congressional Record*.

Thanks to his retentive memory, Bill gradually assimilated a good working knowledge of American politics and he kept a pile of *Congressional Records* for reference. Dimond and his secretary, E.L. (Bob) Bartlett, also kept in touch with Alaskans through local newspapers. Almost every copy of the weekly *Valdez Miner* contained an article about the activities of the delegate and a column by Bartlett.

Egan readily espoused Dimond's political philosophy and affiliation with the Democratic Party. George Sullivan, whose father and mother were politically-active Republicans, recalls political debates with Egan at The Pinzon. Sullivan, who was several years younger than Egan, found Bill to be a capable debater and often had to rely on his mother to provide him with good Republican arguments to counteract Egan's enthusiasm for the New Deal.

Dimond returned to Alaska to campaign prior to the

1934 election even though he was unopposed. His activities during his first term pleased his constituents. He made a policy of criticizing the appointment of non-Alaskans to federal positions in the territory and pushed, unsuccessfully, for the transfer of control over fish and game from federal to territorial management. The New Deal monetary measures led to an increase in the price of gold, which lent new impetus to Alaska mining ventures, and Public Works Administration projects provided work for Alaskans. Although Dimond no longer maintained a residence in Valdez, he visited the city regularly on his trips back to Alaska and Egan enjoyed political discussions with the delegate during these visits.

Dimond's personal style of campaigning, which endeared him to Alaskans, was emulated in subsequent years by both Egan and Bob Bartlett, who served as Dimond's secretary in Washington, D.C., and later replaced him as delegate. Charles Barker recounted his observation of Dimond's campaign technique in an article for *Alaska Life*:

> A very tall man was earnestly talking with a group of business men in the streets of Juneau. He was discussing the complex affairs of the national government at Washington and what was being done to help Alaska. Suddenly, he stepped from the crowd.
>
> "Hello Jimmy, how are you?" He stooped over, extended his hand and a warm smile to a small newsboy. The lad stopped in his tracks, looked up, wonder and amazement in his eyes. "Gee, do you know me, Mr. Dimond? Huh!" "Certainly I do, Jimmy. I knew your mother and father in Valdez quite a few years ago. In fact, I think they met for the first time in my home."
>
> Jimmy's eyes were big as saucers. "And how are your mother and father? Are they well?" "They are fine, Mr.

Dimond. Daddy's got a good job with the A-J. And Mamma's getting fat."

The delegate smiled. "Please give them my best regards, and tell them I'll drop in and say Hello to them before I leave for the Westward." The lad, still in a daze, wandered down South Franklin Street, looked back repeatedly at the tall man who had rejoined the group of business men and again took up the complexities of national legislation.

Had I not seen this bit of drama myself, I would readily discount it as just another one of those multitudinous "humanizing" fairy stories that men in elective positions like to have the hoi-polloi believe. But this incident showed Anthony J. Dimond as Alaskans know him. It spoke more for the genuineness of the man than a dozen vote-getting speeches of most politicians. It registered with the group as indelibly as what he had to tell them about Washington, D.C..

The Democratic Party became increasingly active in Valdez, partly due to the popularity of Tony Dimond and partly because Martin and Margaret Harrais had arrived in town. Martin Harrais, a Democratic old-timer who had previously run for delegate, was appointed U.S. Commissioner for the Valdez precinct. Harrais spoke at a Democratic Jackson Day banquet in January 1936, as did James Patterson, who served in the territorial Legislature. Patterson was greeted with tumultuous applause when he declared that Delegate Dimond had worked harder for the good of Alaska than any of his predecessors and that not only the Democrats but at least 50 percent of the Republicans were behind him as well. At subsequent Democratic functions, Bill Egan was listed as among those in attendance. Martin Harrais died the following year and his wife, Margaret Keenan Harrais, took over as magistrate. Margaret, who had been a school teacher at Fairbanks, McCarthy and Ellamar, became a lifelong friend and advisor to Egan.

Bill Egan was recognized as one of the most eligible young bachelors in Valdez when Neva McKittrick arrived in town in the fall of 1937 to teach at the middle school. Rumors around town had already reported him married on at least one occasion. A newspaper article reported that:

> Pilot Wm. Egan, who has been in Cordova the past week with a broken pipeline and other troubles, all mechanical, arrived in town on the boat last night and will return to Cordova to bring his ship back some time this week. Various telegrams were received from Cordova that Bill was married, in each case the name of the lucky girl being different, so Bill's friends decided either he was a lucky Mormon or the rumors and telegrams were false.

Neva and Bill liked to sing and, in November 1937, they both participated in "a delightful comic operetta" put on by the Choral Club. Bill's friend George Ashby was also in the cast and Ashby's new wife, Katherine, was the stage director. At first Bill was very shy and invited both Neva and a girl friend of her's out on dates together. Neva thought that Bill was really interested in her friend until he bribed one of his boy friends to take the other girl out. According to Neva, the only time Bill lost his shyness was when he was arguing politics. "I had grown up in a Republican family. I hardly knew there was another party. I soon learned never to argue politics with him. I was outclassed. ... Needless to say, he soon began making sense to me. When I first voted in Alaska, he was quite gratified that I registered as a Democrat."

On dates, Bill took Neva driving around town and, on occasion, she reluctantly agreed to fly with him. When the hanger fire in November 1939 destroyed Egan's Aeronica, along with planes owned by the Dieringer

Attractive young teachers like Neva McKittrick enjoyed active social lives in Valdez. She arrived in Valdez in 1937 to teach in the middle school. Here she poses in Native hunting garb for Russell Dow, a member of Bradford Washburn's Mt. Luconia expedition in 1937.—Russell Dow Collection UAA Archives.

brothers and Bob Reeve, Bill did not have the money to buy another one. "I was sorry for him for the financial loss," Neva recalled, "but I always figured that fire saved his life—and maybe mine."

Katherine Ashby, shown here with a child, and her husband George were frequent companions of Bill and Neva Egan during their courtship and early married life.—Russell Dow Collection UAA Archives.

TERRITORIAL POLITICS

The hangar fire that destroyed Bill Egan's Aeronica marked the end of his days as a wild young man. He had already demonstrated his interest in politics by serving on the Valdez City Assembly. When Jimmy Patterson, who had resigned from the territorial Legislature to become federal marshal, approached him to fill out the Democratic ticket for territorial representative in the spring of 1940, Egan was ready to take the next step towards a political career. On April 5, the *Valdez Miner* announced his candidacy and added:

> Mr. Egan is a man who has grown up in Valdez, and therefore is well acquainted with the needs of his division. He is a friend to all and immensely popular in Valdez, as evidenced by his high vote in the municipal election.

Although Egan's district included Anchorage, Seward and Cordova, he did not campaign extensively in the Third Division towns outside Valdez. Instead, he sent out simple cards stating that he was "Born in Alaska, Raised in Alaska, Schooled in Alaska." This was exactly what the voters, who were suspicious of both absentee-owned business and the federal government, wanted to know. He ran well in the April 30 Democratic primary, and easily won a Third Division seat in the territorial House of Representatives in the September general election. Upon learning of Egan's election, Delegate Dimond expressed his pleasure in a letter to his godson:

> It is a distinct pleasure to me to know that you are a member of the legislature and will serve in the House of Representatives during the coming session. I know you will give first-class service and will act upon every question conscientiously and ably.

Prior to attending the legislative session in January 1941, Egan made another important commitment. Under the headline, "Popular Couple Married Quietly Last Saturday", the *Miner* announced:

> Miss Neva McKittrick of Wilson, Kansas, and Mr. William A. Egan of Valdez were united in marriage on Saturday evening at 8:30 at a quiet ceremony at the home of U.S. Commissioner Margaret Harrais. Mr. and Mrs. George Ashby were the only attendants. After the ceremony, Mr. and Mrs. Ashby held open house at their home on Hobart Street for the many friends of the young couple. Later all attended a dance at Hart's.
>
> Miss McKittrick was charmingly attired in a rose colored formal. She has been teaching school in Valdez the last three years and is very popular in the musical and social life of the town.
>
> William Egan, who was born and raised in Valdez, is associated with his brother, C.J. Egan, in the operation of The Pinzon recreational hall and cocktail bar. In the recent territorial election, Mr. Egan was elected one the representatives from the Third Division to the Legislature which will convene in Juneau in January.
>
> Mr. and Mrs. Egan are now at home to their friends in their apartment in the Hart Building on McKinley Street.

Neva remained in Valdez to complete the school term

while Bill departed for Juneau with an agenda that he hoped would advance the cause of statehood for Alaska.

For seven years in Washington, D.C., Delegate Dimond had attempted unsuccessfully to advance Alaskan causes, including the abolition of fish traps, construction of a highway to Alaska, and the establishment of military and naval bases to protect against the threat of Japanese aggression. By 1940 he had determined that "full statehood" was the only answer for the eventual development of Alaska. During visits to his hometown he enlisted Valdezians, including Bill Egan, in the statehood cause. In later years, Egan stated that he owed his enthusiasm for Alaska statehood to Tony Dimond back in Valdez. An article in the *Alaska Frontier*, published in Valdez in January 1941, outlined Dimond's plan:

> Alaska is just as much entitled to statehood as is Hawaii. We'll beat them to it yet if we can. The following steps are necessary to secure a place as the 49th star: (1) presentation by the Territorial Legislature of a petition to Congress voicing the people's request for statehood; (2) passage of an Enabling Act by Congress authorizing the people of Alaska, thru a constitutional convention, to draw up a state constitution; (3) submission of this constitution to the people of the Territory and upon its approval; (4) submission to Congress, whereupon by a resolution of that body, the Territory can be declared to be a State.

The newspaper article stressed that the first step in securing statehood was thus up to the Legislature of Alaska, and that the Legislature would be convening in January.

The first bill that Representative Bill Egan presented at the 1941 legislative session was one authorizing a statewide referendum on statehood. When Representative Allan Shattuck questioned whether Alaska could assume the expenses of statehood, Egan responded that Delegate Dimond, who was thoroughly conversant with territorial affairs, was definitely in favor of giving Alaskans an opportunity to vote on the question. The bill easily passed in the House of Representatives, but was narrowly defeated in the Senate. Other legislation introduced by Egan during the session related to local Valdez and Copper River area concerns, which included memorials urging the federal government to replace the

Bill Egan, back row third from the right, served in the 1941 Alaska Territorial Legislature, presided over by H.H. McCutcheon.—CC8576, Steve McCutcheon Collection, AMHA.

Valdez courthouse that burned in December 1940, to construct a new hospital for Valdez, and to build a highway along the corridor abandoned by the Copper River and Northwestern Railway.

Egan was appointed to standing committees on Ways and Means, Fisheries, Mining and Manufacturing, and Roads and Highways. During this session, testimony before the Mining and Manufacturing committee about the potential oil reserves in northern Alaska convinced Egan that "petroleum would make Alaska."

During the 1941 Legislature, Egan met Governor Ernest Gruening and Secretary of State E.L. (Bob) Bartlett, two men that would be associated with him in years to come as Alaska fought for statehood. Bartlett, the son of a Fairbanks miner, came from an Alaskan background similar to Egan's. He had given up mining to serve as Dimond's

Secretary of Alaska E.L. (Bob) Bartlett, shown addressing a crowd on Labor Day 1941, joined Bill Egan in advocating statehood for Alaska.—MCC005, Steve McCutcheon Collection, AMHA.

secretary when Dimond became delegate in 1932. Dimond had subsequently been influential in Bartlett's appointment as Alaska's secretary of state. Governor Gruening, on the other hand, was from a wealthy New York Jewish family. He had graduated from Harvard University with a medical degree, but chose a career in journalism and politics instead of practicing medicine. Gruening deliberatively singled Egan out as a progressive young legislator who could support his administrative policies according to Katie Hurley, who was Gruening's secretary at the time. Egan did support Governor Gruening's unsuccessful attempt in 1941 to adopt a tax structure that would generate more funds for development in Alaska and demonstrate to the federal government that Alaska was ready to assume more financial responsibility.

Gruening's appointment in 1939 to replace Governor John W. Troy had not been popular with Alaskans, who agreed with Delegate Dimond that the governor of Alaska should be an Alaskan. Furthermore, Gruening had been director of territories and island possessions in the Interior Department under Interior Secretary Harold Ickes, who was universally disliked in Alaska. Even though Gruening often opposed Ickes' policies, he still represented the Interior Department to many Alaskans. As secretary of state, Bartlett frequently served as acting governor when Gruening, who maintained a home and close connections in Washington, D.C., was away from his Juneau office. Bartlett was a close personal friend of the Dimond family, and, like Egan, was an early convert to the cause of statehood.

Egan was convinced from the beginning that Gruening was what Alaska needed to stand up to absentee owners of fisheries and mines. Although he generally sided with Governor Gruening in matters relating to taxes, New Deal programs, and human rights, Egan followed Delegate Dimond's lead when it came to some local issues like the eagle bounty. After Dimond had succeeded in exempting Alaska from the National Eagle Protection Act, Egan, as president of Eagle Aerie No.1971 in Valdez, received pleas from Audubon Societies and stateside aeries of the Fraternal Order of Eagles that he introduce a bill to repeal the Alaska bounty law. Dimond had introduced the eagle bounty when he was in the Alaska Legislature at the request of Prince William Sound fox farmers because eagles were attacking their young foxes. In a lengthy response to one of these requests, Egan explained:

> Alaska, in her delegate to Congress, Mr. Anthony J. Dimond, Past President of Valdez Aerie No.1971, Fraternal Order of Eagles, has a man who understands and has traversed nearly all of Alaska. To imply that our delegate "slipped" in an amendment to the National Eagle Bill, is making an unjust statement. Mr. Dimond "fought" for the amendment. He fought for it because he understands the problem of Alaska as regards the measure.

In his first message to the Alaska Legislature in January 1941, Gruening pointed out that it would seem reasonable for Alaska to move in the direction established elsewhere in the country and at least cease paying a bounty on the national bird. When a bill to repeal the eagle bounty was introduced in the Alaska Senate, Egan was called upon to testify and his spirited defense of the eagle bounty was sufficient to kill the repeal measure. Egan thus earned the nickname "Eagle Bounty Bill". Although he succeeded in killing the bounty repeal in 1941, money for paying the bounty was vetoed by the governor. Gruening continued to press for repeal, but was not successful until 1945 when Egan was no longer in the Legislature.

On March 28, Egan, as the youngest member of the Legislature, made the traditional final motion of the session soon after the House of Representatives received word that the Senate had completed their business. Serving in the Legislature was a learning experience for Egan and an opportunity to broaden his horizons. His friend from Valdez, Margaret Keenan Harrais, was in Juneau during the session as a member of the Territorial Board of Education. She claimed in later years to have taught Egan parliamentary procedure, possibly during this legislative session.

Magistrate Margaret Keenan Harrais in front of her Valdez home. Egan and Bartlett visited her whenever they were in Valdez. She claimed to have given Bob Bartlett his first spanking (For shooting craps in school.), and to have taught Bill Egan parliamentary procedures.—Clifton Collection UAF Archives.

Upon return to Valdez, Egan realized that his hometown was becoming more isolated. Hal Selby, the editor of the *Valdez Miner* had died and his son was planning to move the printing equipment to Juneau. Valdez would no longer have a newspaper or a courthouse. After the old court house burned, the seat of the Third Division was moved to Anchorage. Valdez students would no longer be able to profit from these institutions that broadened the education of Egan and his contemporaries. Although he could not replace these losses, Egan shared his Juneau experience in an address to Valdez High School students about the making of legislation in the territorial Legislature.

Meanwhile in Washington, D.C., Delegate Dimond was introducing House Resolution No. 142 asking that the House Committee on Territories make an investigation of questions relative to the matter of statehood for the territory, including the fitness of Alaska to undertake the burdens of state government. On April 17 Dimond introduced H.R.4397 to amend the Organic Act of Alaska to provide for reallocation of the Alaska Territorial Legislature on a population base. No action was taken on these measures during the 1941 Congressional sessions.

In December 1941 the United States went to war and Bill and Neva Egan had a baby daughter, Elin Carol, born in Valdez by Caesarian section. The war effort increased activity at the Valdez dock and on the Richardson Highway. In addition to his duties at The Pinzon bar, Bill worked on the dock unloading construction material for airfields and highway improvements. Tragedy struck in July 1942 when the Egans' 7-month-old baby girl died, possibly as a result of pyloric stenosis. Egan did not seek reelection to the Valdez City Council in 1942 but ran successfully for another term as representative from the Third Division.

Neva accompanied Bill when he returned to Juneau in

January for the 1943 legislative session. The Legislature adjourned on March 25 after a relatively uneventful session during which Egan again introduced a bill authorizing a statewide referendum on statehood, sought federal appropriation for the construction of a federal building in Valdez with a courthouse and jail, and state funding for the eagle bounty.

Although the 1943 Legislature did not support his bill for a referendum, statehood was still foremost in Egan's mind. Upon his return to Valdez, he wrote the following editorial, which was printed in one of the last issues of the *Valdez Miner* on April 23:

> The most momentous measure ever effecting the great Territory of Alaska and all Alaskans has apparently received little worthwhile recognition by either the newspapers or the residents of the Territory.
>
> Referred to is the resolution introduced in the United States Senate April 7 by Senator William Langer (Republican, North Dakota) and Senator Pat McCarron (Democrat, Nevada). The resolution calls for a congressional Enabling Act taking Alaska into the Union as the Forty-ninth State, and establishing district court headquarters at Juneau, Nome, Valdez and Fairbanks.
>
> If Congress should pass the resolution (and there is every indication that Congress will) then the people of the Territory of Alaska would have placed before them on a ballot either at a special or general election, the question of ratification of the Constitution of the Forty-ninth state —ALASKA.
>
> It is our opinion that Alaska's citizens, as a whole, have never given serious consideration to the question of Statehood. Most of us have proceeded on the assumption that it would be a great honor to have our flag's forty-ninth star added in our recognition, but, without further serious investigation, have let the matter drop.

Greatest single objection to Alaska's Statehood in the minds of those Alaskans who have spent no time in real approachment to the question, is the defeatist attitude that the Territory would not have the finances to carry the burden of Statehood. In answer to this feeling we say rather bluntly that there is no slight foundation for any such fear.

What has been the cry of Alaskans for decades? At whom have we thrown stones? We have cried that the absence of anything approximating complete home rule in the Territory has seriously hampered our industrial progress. We have cried that bureaucrats in Washington, D.C., who know little or practically nothing of the peculiarities affecting Alaskan industry have held a hot iron over our advancements. We have cried that these men have too freely and too often brandished this iron—the iron of absentee power. We have seen a perpetual industrial potentiality, namely the Southeastern Alaska pulp lands—refused the right of operation because Federal Reserve Land restrictions would place a company's millions of dollars of invested capital in jeopardy in a very few years. We have noted that whenever the presence of oil was discovered in a locality, Federal Reserve Land restrictions placed the investment of large capital in jeopardy. The same applies to our large coal fields; in some instances to our mining ground. And what have we, as a people of a Territory, got to say about it? Nothing, Mr. and Mrs. Citizen, nothing.

Remember that when Alaska becomes a state, (and Alaska will become a state) YOU will have two United States Senators and at least one Representative in the United States Congress. Remember that they will be VOTING Senators and VOTING Representatives. Remember that YOU will then have a DIRECT voice in national affairs yourself, and remember that the State of Alaska will share proportionally in ALL appropriations made in favor of the many states by YOUR Federal Government.

> The day is coming in the not-too-distant future when YOU will go to the polls and cast your ballot on the ratification of the Constitution for the State of Alaska. Results of your unified actions on that day will determine whether or not Alaskans were sincere in the many long, hard-fought battles of years past in which "Home Rule" was the battle cry.

Delegate Dimond had been instrumental in persuading Senators Langer and McCarron to introduce an Alaska Statehood Bill in the Senate and, the following December, he submitted his own companion bill, H.R.951, which was similar to the Senate bill. Dimond was not as optimistic as young Bill Egan about prompt consideration of Alaska statehood while World War II was the primary national consideration, but he wanted to open discussion of the concept both in Congress and in Alaska.

POST-WAR TERRITORIAL LEGISLATURE

As a member of the territorial Legislature, Bill Egan could have been deferred from military service in World War II, but he still was fasci-

Sgt. William A. Egan served in the Army Aircorps Quartermaster Corps at Ladd Field in Fairbanks from 1944 to 1946.—Photo courtesy of Gerald Bowkett.

nated by airplanes and anxious to join the Air Force. Soon after he returned to Valdez after the 1943 legislative session, the *Miner* announced: "After a few weeks at home, Bill Egan left Wednesday for Fairbanks where he will endeavor to enlist in the Air Corps." This attempt misfired. He was inducted as a private in the Army instead and sent to boot camp. Army riflery training exercises presented Egan with unexpected difficulties because he was forced to use right-handed equipment even though he was left handed and proficient in shooting from that side. Eventually, through the intercession of Governor Gruening, Egan was transferred to the Army Air Corps and assigned to Ladd Field in Fairbanks. He was considered too old at 29 for flight training even though he had been a private pilot. He was assigned instead to the quartermaster service where his excellent memory for details soon made him indispensable. At a personal level, this assignment was fortuitous. He was allowed to live in town permitting Neva to join him in Fairbanks, where she was employed by a local bank.

The years spent in military service provided a respite from his political career, but his Fairbanks assignment helped Egan form valuable political contacts. Territorial Senator John Butrovich and his wife became good friends of the Egans, and the friendship endured through the years even though Butrovich and Egan were in different political parties and found themselves running against each other in a later election. Egan's friendship with E.L. (Bob) Bartlett flourished while Bartlett was running for delegate to Congress in 1944. Although they had known each other during the legislative sessions in Juneau, it was in Fairbanks that they became close friends and associates in the fight for Alaska statehood.

In 1943, with the question of statehood slowly moving up on the agenda for both Congress and the people of Alaska, Delegate Dimond wrote Bartlett a confidential letter indicating that he was considering not running for another term as delegate and suggesting Bartlett run in his place. Dimond was 63 years old and repeated surgeries on his crippled leg as well as a pulmonary embolism were draining his ability to face the stress of Washington life. When Bartlett repeated this information to Gruening, the governor was pleased to add his encouragement to a Bartlett candidacy. Gruening and Dimond had not always agreed and Gruening thought he would have an easier time influencing Bartlett. Since Dimond had voiced an interest in being a federal judge, Gruening did what he could to see that Dimond received such an appointment.

Bartlett, like Egan, joined Dimond in ardently supporting the statehood cause. During a speech in Wrangell, Bartlett came out unequivocally for statehood much to the discomfort of Governor Gruening, who, according to Vide Bartlett, characterized statehood at that time as a "mad, wild, and impossible idea that nobody wanted." Although Gruening did not believe that Bartlett could be elected if he campaigned on a statehood plank, Alaskans proved him wrong. Bartlett succeeded Dimond, who accepted a federal judicial appointment to the Third Division court, which had been moved to Anchorage from Valdez.

By the time the 1945 territorial Legislature met in Juneau, Dimond's attempts to get better population representation had been successful. With increased representation from the rapidly growing areas of Alaska, the territorial Legislature finally passed a bill authorizing a statewide referendum on statehood, which passed with a vote of 9,630 in favor as opposed to 6,822 against. With this definite, though not overwhelming, affirmation of the desire for statehood, Governor Gruening joined the outspoken statehood advocates.

Bill Egan missed the 1945 legislative session because he

was still in military service. The citizens of Valdez, however, anticipated his discharge. When he returned to Valdez in 1946, he found that they had already elected him mayor. Egan took advantage of the generous loan program for returning veterans and joined his friend Joe Dieringer in establishing a grocery business in Valdez.

Egan's new business responsibilities in Valdez were not sufficient to keep him from continuing his political career. He was back as a Third Division representative when the Eighteenth Territorial Legislature opened in January 1947. Governor Gruening promptly introduced comprehensive measures, taxing both income and property in hope that the Legislature, which had a population-based House membership, would be more receptive to taxes than it had been before the war. Egan, as well as some of the other returning veterans, supported the governor's efforts to make Alaska more self-supporting, recognizing that the burgeoning postwar population would make increased demands on the government.. Since the conservative Senate balked at passing such comprehensive measures, the House resorted to enacting lesser taxes dedicated to supporting construction of facilities such as hospitals.

Although Egan was hoping to get funding for a Valdez hospital, he protested against a lottery tax that another Democratic representative, Steve McCutcheon from Anchorage, introduced as a stopgap measure. McCutcheon, another Alaska-born young veteran, who had been appointed in 1945 to complete the Senate term of his deceased father, was released by the Army to serve in the 1946 Special Session of the Legislature. Egan, who had seniority as a result of his prewar legislative experience, resented McCutcheon's attempts to "dominate the House." Egan was reported in the Juneau newspaper as saying, "Mr. McCutcheon is constantly directing sneering remarks toward other members of the House and attempting to insult them and belittle their rights as members to do whatever they think best for the people of Alaska. I resent this, not only when it is directed at myself but when it is aimed at any other member. Mr. McCutcheon forgets that the voters elected 24 representatives to this House; he wants to run the whole thing himself." When Egan finished, he drew a round of applause from the House members, including McCutcheon himself. Although the *Anchorage Times* speculated that this episode might indicate a split among the progressive, pro-administration legislators, both Egan and McCutcheon continued to support Governor Gruening in his attempt to change the tax structure of the territory. In spite of their efforts, the Eighteenth Session adamantly refused to endorse the new taxes and adjourned without appropriating enough money to support the government for two years.

The Eighteenth Session was an especially memorable one for the Egans. Neva had accompanied Bill to Juneau and, on March 3, 1947, their son was delivered by Caesarian section. The official *Territorial House Journal* recorded the birth of the new Egan son: "A new `Bill' by Mr. Egan, presented by Mrs. Egan, arrived at 9:55 o'clock, a.m., March 3, 1947, entitled `Dennis William Egan.'"

Governor Gruening called for a special session of the territorial Legislature to meet immediately preceding the Nineteenth Session in January 1949. Since the new Legislature would include two new senators and 14 new representatives, the governor hoped that a solution could be reached to Alaska's financial crisis. The editor of the Juneau paper described what he termed "one of the biggest messes to confront lawmakers for many a year" Theoretically, Alaska's government was forbidden by law to incur debt. However, it was facing a deficit approaching a million dollars and on top of the deficit was requesting $17,500,000 for the next biennium - about twice the amount appropriated for the last two years.

Democrats had been supportive of the governor's tax proposals in the 1947 session and, since six of the eight

Bill Egan with son Dennis, born in Juneau during the 1947 territorial legislative session.—Photo courtesy of Gerald Bowkett.

senators and 19 of the 24 representative were Democrats, chances seemed good that new taxes would be instituted. The House went to work promptly and halfway through the 17-day Extraordinary Session of the Nineteenth Legislature had already introduced 10 bills, eight of which dealt with revenue measures. The bill authorizing a net income tax was quickly passed on to the Senate. By the time the Nineteenth Legislature adjourned on March 24, the following revenue measures had been passed: Property Tax—HB2 levied a tax of 10 mills on real and personal property to be refunded to municipalities and school districts; Raw Fish Tax—HB3 levied a tax

Territorial Governor Ernest Gruening signing bills that created a tax structure for Alaska in 1949 with Stanley McCutcheon, left, and Victor Rivers, center.—Steve McCutcheon Collection, AMHA.

of one percent on the value of halibut, salmon and other fish and two percent on shellfish; Fish Trap Tax—HB4 quadrupled the former license tax on fish traps; Fishermen's Licenses—HB7 increased the rate of commercial fishermen's licenses; Business Licenses— HB10 imposed a basic business license fee; Income Tax—HB92 levied a tax on net income amounting to 10 per cent of the tax paid to the Federal government; Tobacco Tax— HB53 imposed a tax on cigarettes, cigars, and tobacco; Punch Board Tax—HB71 imposed a license tax of $2 on punch boards. In addition, HB65 enabled municipalities to levy sales taxes of up to two per cent if approved by 55 per cent of voters within the municipality. The Democrats had met the fiscal crisis head on.

While all of these tax measures were under consideration, Egan attempted to introject some comic relief by proposing a tax on single women, which stimulated a barrage of comment from all over the country. After reading an article in the *Chicago Daily News* about Egan's bill calling for a $50 head tax on single women, Adele E. Brunzell complained:

> I'm wondering if this Bill might be for the purpose of "scaring" whatever eligible single women there might be in Alaska into marrying eligible single men, some of these women in "these days and times" probably considering it a luxury to be single, or is it this particular "luxury" that is taxable? In all seriousness, have you ever made a survey of HOW MUCH single women contribute in doing things for their families and relatives, and also that a single person pays more in the way of income tax? If single women are to be taxed, how about single men? Anyway, as it is at present with income tax, sales tax, luxury tax, amusement tax, etc., we'll probably soon be taxed for the air we breathe! ... Personally, as an American citizen, I regard such a Bill as UNFAIR.

Needless to say the Alaska Legislature did not choose to enact a tax on single women.

During the Nineteenth Legislature, Egan chaired the Municipal Affairs Committee and also served on Elections, Election Laws and Mileage; Roads and Highways; Transportation, Commerce and Navigation; Veteran's Legislation; and Ways and Means. Speaker of the House Stanley McCutcheon frequently had Egan preside over the House so that he could participate more actively in the floor discussions.

Since the territory's fiscal crisis, which had been an argument against statehood, was alleviated by the new tax measures, the Nineteenth Legislature addressed the statehood question by creating the Alaska Statehood Committee. Twenty-one members were to be appointed to assemble material, make studies, and provide recommendations for a statehood convention to frame a state constitution. Egan, who was presiding over the House when efforts were made to block consideration of the bill creating the Statehood Committee, ruled that the bill could be discussed and acted upon. Statehood was foremost in the minds of the legislators during the 1949 legislative session because bills approving statehood for both Alaska and Hawaii were being discussed in Washington, D.C. Early in the session the Third Division legislators held a caucus to discuss statehood strategies. At this caucus they discussed the advisability of holding a convention to draft a constitution even if no congressional action was taken that year advancing Alaska statehood.

In March 1950, the Democrats demonstrated their confidence in Egan's leadership by electing him to succeed Stanley McCutcheon as chairman of their Third Division committee. The chairmanship allowed Egan to make recommendations to Delegate Bartlett about patronage appointments of officials such as postmasters in the various Third Division towns, and occasionally made it necessary for him to settle conflicts within the Party. In a personal letter to Egan on January 17, 1951, Bartlett commented:

> I really feel sorry for you in the difficulties you have had
> and at the same time have a fellow feeling for you. A care-
> ful reading of your letters is bound to lead one to the abso-
> lute conclusion that you acted properly in the Seward
> matter. If you erred at all, it was in the direction of waiting
> too long for advices from Anchorage and that is the same
> kind of an error I should have made. Actually, there is a
> need on the part of some of the Third Division members
> to realize that the other communities of the Third Division
> have a responsible stake in all of this, and that the head
> and the feet and everything in between aren't located in
> Anchorage. ... To sum it up, let me say that I have been
> delighted with your splendid cooperation as chairman. The
> party throughout the Third Division should be likewise
> delighted and should applaud your actions instead of try-
> ing to carp at episodes such as the Seward one.

When the Twentieth Legislature assembled in January 1951,
Egan was elected speaker of the House. Stanley McCutcheon continued to be the Democratic floor leader and was
prepared to use his majority position to still the voices of
opposition. Egan, however, insisted on strict adherence to
parliamentary procedure and nonpartisan fairness. During the final evening session Speaker Egan was presented
with a painting of Mt. McKinley as a token of appreciation
for "a job well done." Egan was chosen to fill one of the
four places on the reconstituted Board of Administration,
as provided in the Government Reorganization Bill that
passed the Legislature during the final session. Delegate
Bartlett noted Egan's success, writing him in Valdez after
the close of the legislative session:

> From many different quarters I have heard flattering com-
> ments about your work in the Legislature, both as an in-
> dividual member and as speaker of the House. Everyone
> has referred to you in glowing terms, and I want to add
> my heartiest congratulations.

Egan's decision to run for the territorial Senate in 1952 was applauded by Steve McCutcheon, who was also running for Senate on the Democratic ticket, and by Delegate Bartlett. Bartlett's prediction that Egan would be a sure winner was correct, but otherwise the Democrats fared poorly in the election where Dwight David Eisenhower defeated Adlai Stevenson for president. Alaska Republicans won clear majorities in both the House and

Speaker William A. Egan presided over the territorial House of Representatives in 1951.—Photo courtesy of Gerald Bowkett.

the Senate. Steve McCutcheon, who was one of the defeated Democrats wrote Egan:

> Thanks for your note of condolence—frankly I'm happy as hell that it happened that way. I think that you can do better in the Senate than either of we McCutcheons, because we have been under fire so much

from not only elements of our own party but the opposition party. Further, you are much more of a diplomat than I and I am sure will be able to exercise much more influence, than my aggressive slashing tactics could possibly avail.

Delegate Bartlett was reelected in the 1952 election in a close contest with Egan's former pilot and employer, Bob

Governor Gruening's wife, Dorothy, serves punch to Neva Egan during a reception for legislators and their wives.— Anchorage Museum of History and Art.

Reeve, the Republican candidate. In a letter congratulating Egan on his election, Bartlett analyzed the situation:

The reasons you were elected when our other people fell by the wayside are not too difficult to discover. They have something to do with obvious sincerity and integrity and ability. ... Allow me to say further that there was no man running for office in all of Alaska who I would rather have seen win than you. I mean that.

The Twenty-First Legislature was contentious because Governor Gruening was temporarily permitted to stay in office to the dismay of the Republican-dominated Legislature, which did everything it could to alter the progressive tax proposals that had passed in 1949. As one of the few Democrats in the Senate, Egan had little influence. When the session ended, the territorial government was underfunded again.

When the Twenty-Second Legislature convened in January 1955, the situation was completely reversed. Alaska Democrats had fared well in the 1954 election, in part because President Eisenhower had not supported Alaska statehood while President Truman and the Democratic administration had been receptive. The Democrats won a 12 to 4 majority in the Alaska Senate and a 21 to 3 majority in the House. The contention during this session was between the Democratic House majority and Republican Governor Heintzleman, who had by then been appointed to replace Gruening.

The Democrats criticized the governor for not obtaining a federal loan to bolster the unemployment compensation fund. The Legislature adjourned without passing a budget and demanded that the governor call a special session to deal with unemployment compensation. Unemployment compensation favored the construction industry over the fishing industry and some of the more conservative senators, both Democrats and Republicans favored better compensation for fishermen. During the special session, the House leadership under Stanley Mc-Cutcheon and Speaker Wendell Kay was blamed for the continued contention in a Juneau editorial:

> It is evident and clear-cut that the well-being of Alaska, the efficient operation of government, the dignity that is supposed to be inherent in legislators has been cast aside by majority Democrats. Substituted for the normal behavior of lawmakers has been an attempt to "get" Governor Heintzleman and his administration, and legislators have summoned every street corner tactic at their command.

Egan, who was serving in the Senate, escaped the venom directed at the Third Division Democrats in the House, although he generally supported the House's stand on unemployment compensation. Eventually the House Democrats split and a compromise was agreed upon, but bitterness lingered.

In contrast to the fight over unemployment compensation, a bill passed easily authorizing a constitutional convention to be held at the University of Alaska in Fairbanks in November 1955. Delegates to the convention were to be elected both on a regional basis and at-large. Egan was excited about a constitutional convention and enjoyed his legislative duties but business came first and he decided not a run for either the convention or the legislature. Neva and Dennis had accompanied Egan to Juneau for the 1953 session. Later that year the Egans bought out their partner in Valdez Supply, obliging Neva to stay in Valdez to run the store. Egan knew that he would have to make a decision between politics and his Valdez business.

CONSTITUTIONAL CONVENTION

Bill Egan returned to Valdez after the 1955 legislative session convinced that his future commitment would be to the grocery business in Valdez. Neva had been forced to stay in Valdez to manage the store after the Egans bought out their partner, Joe Dieringer.

Valdez Supply, Egan's Valdez store that Neva had to run while Bill was participating in the 1955 territorial Legislature.—Photo courtesy of Gerald Bowkett.

Years later Neva recalled her discomfort while running the store that winter in an interview with John Whitehead, a University of Alaska history professor:

> It wasn't as easy for me to do it alone as it was with both of us because he (Bill) hauled the freight from the dock and he did everything. ... I didn't help him—he was the owner, he did things. Then when he was gone, suddenly there I was, having to do it. And then Dennis was a little fellow. Finally, we decided he was either in business or he was in politics, he had to decide. He decided that, in order to make a go of our store and to build it up as we wanted to ... he would just have to get out of politics, at least for a while and take care of the store.

Assuming that he would not be taking part in the constitutional convention in November 1955, Egan encouraged his friend Tommy Harris to file for convention delegate from the Valdez district.

During the 1955 Legislature, Egan, as chairman of the Senate Committee on Statehood and National Relations, was responsible for drafting the legislation calling for the constitutional convention. His counterpart in the House, Representative Thomas Stewart of Juneau, traveled around the country collecting information to help in drafting the convention legislation. They worked together as a joint committee with Stewart as chairman. Although previous statehood enabling bills called for using the existing legislative districting structure for the election of convention delegates, the joint committee decided on a new scheme to assure as equitable territory-wide participation as possible. They fixed the number of delegates at 55—the same number that drafted the United States Constitution. Seven delegates were to be selected at large from the whole territory to balance the sectionalism expected to arise among selections from the four territorial judicial districts. Having at-large seats would encourage the most prominent residents of the territory to file as candidates. The remaining 48 delegates were to be elected on a regional basis. To prevent domination by the urban areas, 15 delegates were to be elected from newly delineated single-delegate districts, like Valdez, that were not related to population.

As the filing date for the September 13 special election drew near, friends urged Egan to file and he, undoubtedly, began to regret that he would not be part of the convention that he helped plan. Finally he was persuaded to file for one of the at-large seats since he didn't want to compete with his friend Thomas Harris for the Valdez seat. The Sunday before the filing deadline Egan went around town in Valdez to get his petition signed and then flew to Anchorage to file, uncertain of the reliability of the mail. Egan's legislative role made him sufficiently well known throughout the territory to win an at-large seat for the convention. His understanding with Neva was that this would be his last political activity and that running the business in Valdez would be his priority.

The joint planning committee of the 1955 Legislature decided that the convention should take place on the campus of the University of Alaska at College, near Fairbanks, rather than in Juneau, attracted by the academic setting rather than the political atmosphere of the capital. The committee also designated a 75-day convention broken by a recess during which the delegates could return home and talk with their constituents. An appropriation of $300,000 from the territorial Legislature enabled hiring staff and securing the service of consultants.

The decision to hold the convention in Fairbanks during the winter was considered advantageous because the delegates would have few activities to distract them. However, midwinter transportation to Fairbanks presented problems for delegates from some of the more remote areas. Burke Riley, a delegate from Haines, drove up alone a week before the convention was due to start, shoveling snow in advance as he approached the summit on the Haines Highway. He had served in the 1955 Legislature and was convinced that Egan should preside at the convention. Upon arrival in Fairbanks, he met George McLaughlin, an attorney from Anchorage, who had inde-

Delegates to the Alaska Constitutional Convention were geographically representative of the non-Native population of Alaska.—MCC#19208, Steve McCutcheon Collection, AMHA.

pendently come to the same conclusion. They met other delegates arriving in Fairbanks, including Victor Fischer and Barrie White, Operation Statehood officers from Anchorage. They felt that Egan had the right temperament to lead the convention in addition to knowledge of parliamentary procedure. Although Victor Rivers, a civil engineer and long-term legislator from Anchorage and his brother Ralph from Fairbanks were openly seeking the position, few delegates had committed themselves. Most delegates had little opportunity before the convention to discuss leadership alternatives so the presidency was still wide open as the delegates trickled in to Fairbanks.

Bill Egan did not arrive in Fairbanks until the day before the convention. Since it was difficult to get in and out of Valdez during the winter, he hitched a ride on a big truck that was delivering freight to Fairbanks. Burke Riley and several other delegates greeted Egan as he jumped out of the truck and took him to meet Bob Bartlett in his makeshift office in the Fairbanks federal building to discuss organization of the convention. Although Egan had no prior intention of campaigning for the presidency, they convinced him to let his name be placed in nomination.

The delegates to the constitutional convention were geographically representative of the non-Native population of the time. Thirty-one were from Alaska's three major cities (Anchorage, Fairbanks, and Juneau), the remaining 24 came from 19 communities widely dispersed throughout the territory, from the Bering Sea to Ketchikan. Ages of delegates ranged from 29 to 82 years old. They represented a variety of occupations: 13 lawyers, 20 businessmen, 40 miners, three commercial fishermen, six professionals, three housewives, and a homesteader. Only one, Frank Peratrovich, a Tlingit Indian, was a Native Alaskan, although eight were Alaska-born. Thirty delegates had held a variety of current and previous elective offices, 16 in the territorial legislature. Only ten delegates had no prior service in a public office.

The constitutional convention opened in the University

of Alaska gymnasium on November 8, 1955 with great formality and enthusiasm. Welcoming statements were delivered by University President Ernest N. Patty, Delegate Bartlett, former Governor Ernest Gruening, and Robert B. Atwood, chairman of the Alaska Statehood Committee. Years later, Egan recalled that day: "I remember well the atmosphere of the convention, a feeling that we were working on something that would have an everlasting impact on the future of the then Territory of Alaska and the new state-to-be. There was a feeling of something historic, of something that just had to be accomplished in a given period of time."

After the introductory speeches, the delegates elected a temporary chairman. The two nominations for the position were Mildred Hermann, member of the Alaska Statehood Committee often referred to as "the grand old lady of Alaska statehood," and William A. Egan. In their enthusiasm to have Egan chair the convention, some of the novices supported Egan, but the more experienced political leaders recognized that the temporary chairmanship was mainly ceremonial and elected Mrs. Hermann as chairman pro tem. Burke Riley recalled that Egan voted for himself by mistake—"It was the only time Egan was flustered."

Four candidates were nominated for convention president. E.B. Collins, an 82-year-old Fairbanks attorney, had been speaker of the House of Representatives during the First Alaska Legislature in 1913. Ralph J. Rivers had served as elected attorney general of Alaska and as mayor of Fairbanks. His brother Victor C. Rivers was a territorial senator and member of the Alaska Statehood Committee. Egan was nominated by John Rosswog of Cordova. Eventually, the choice of convention president came down to the personalities of the two leading contenders, Victor Rivers and Egan. Rivers was the more forceful but his strong personality contributed to his eventual defeat. Egan was gentle and soft-spoken, with a style that influenced people through persuasion and a search for consensus. The delegates, particularly those with no previous legislative experience, were looking for a president who would be fair and impartial. They felt more comfortable with Egan and elected him convention president on the third ballot.

Constitutional Convention President William A. Egan with staff, Secretary Thomas Stewart and Chief Clerk Katie Alexander.—MCC#006, Steve McCutcheon, AMHA.

Egan did not disappoint his followers. In his book on the constitutional convention, Delegate Victor Fischer described Egan's handling of the convention:

> Most important was Convention President Egan's gentle touch and parliamentary knowledge. Whenever complex issues arose that could not be readily resolved by floor de-

bate, or if tensions or misunderstandings began to develop, he would call a recess during which matters could be resolved and mutually satisfactory changes drafted. In these instances, which sometimes occurred many times a day, Egan would leave the matter to those directly concerned; only when he felt his personal intervention was important would he participate in the discussion. Procedural strictures in convention rules were resorted to only in extreme circumstances. Egan demonstrated a remarkable sense of tim-

Delegates confer informally with Convention President Egan, seated. Standing left to right John Hellenthal, George McLaughlin, Robert McNealy, Leslie Nerland, Steve Mc-Cutcheon, John Coghill, Clerk Katie Alexander, John Cress, Dorothy Awes. —MCC#25643, Steve McCutcheon Collection, AMHA.

ing and judgment that made him appear completely patient when patience was required or extremely urgent when speedy agreement was a necessity. He knew how to apply the rules of procedure to produce the widest consensus and how to use good sense, humor, and sympathy to smooth out difficulties. He helped inexperienced delegates over rough spots and gradually welded a group of extreme individualists into a thoroughly effective working body. Occasional personal conflicts and disagreements were not allowed to divide the convention leadership, and adequate rules of procedure combined to ensure a successful convention.

Fischer described one example of how Egan defused an incipient conflict by interrupting a heated discussion to inform the delegates that the temperature outside was well below zero and they had better check their vehicles. When the delegates returned they had cooled down enough to resolve the conflict.

The convention established eleven substantive com-

Constitutional convention in plenary session with President Egan presiding.—MCC#009, Steve McCutcheon Collection, AMHA.

mittees: Preamble and Bill of Rights; Suffrage, Elections, and Apportionment; Legislative Branch; Executive Branch; Judiciary Branch; Resources; Finance and Taxation; Local Government; Direct Legislation, Amendment, and Revision; Resolutions and Recommendation; and Ordinances and Transitional Measures. In addition they formed three nonsubstantive committees: Rules; Administration; and Style and Drafting. Each convention delegate, except the president, was appointed to at least one but no more than three standing committees. Always aware of the threat of sectionalism, President Egan chose a representative advisory group to help him make committee selections. Each delegate was given the opportunity to state three choices for committee assignment and generally received appointments reflecting his choices. Committee chairmen were selected by the president to represent various geographical areas and both political parties. Egan announced his appointments on the fifth convention day. Newcomers to public affairs as well as experienced legislators received chairmanships, but

Constitutional convention consultants with Secretary Thomas Stewart, standing. Seated, left to right, Emil Sady, Public Administration Service; J. Kimbrough Owen, Louisiana State University; John Bebout, assistant director National Municipal League.—MCC#25664, Steve McCutcheon Collection, AMHA.

Egan did not allow anyone who represented an extreme position to be a committee chairman. After all appointments were made, Egan called a meeting of committee chairmen, thus creating an informal steering committee for the convention. An article in the *Fairbanks Daily News-Miner* reported Egan as saying: "All delegates stand willing to accept whatever task is given them and they are not inserting any of their ambitions or political beliefs in the proceedings."

The convention committees were assisted in their work by a panel of consultants assembled from universities in Florida, Virginia, Colorado, Oregon, and Louisiana in addition to Alaska. Through these consultants, the delegates were able to obtain advice from widely recognized national authorities on state and local government. Advisors were assigned by Egan after Convention Secretary Thomas Stewart met with each group to review their needs. Eventually, all committees but Rules used consultants.

A heavy schedule of social activities greeted the delegates. They were guests of honor at public receptions and in private homes. Egan and several other delegates rented apartments in the Polaris building. In a November 23 letter to Neva back in Valdez, Egan described some of the social activities and also commented with satisfaction on the reception he was receiving in Fairbanks:

> Was out to the Bartlett's for dinner last nite. There were quite a number there—Burke Riley, George Sundborg, Katherine Alexander, Truman Emberg, H.R. Vanderleest, John Hellenthal, and Jack Hinkle. They had a sort of buffet dinner and I guess it was close to midnite when we got home. Ed Davis (a wonderful person) and John Hellenthal have apartments alongside of mine. The Marstons are down the hall just beyond Davis, and Mrs. Marston had me in to breakfast every morning till I got so embarrassed at accepting their hospitality that I just refused to go any more. Ha! Maybe I shouldn't say anything about this, but Bill Snedden, the publisher of the Newsminer, told Bob Bartlett that beginning soon he was going to start slanting a lot of his columns toward Bill

Egan because he is convinced Bill Egan should be the first governor of the State of Alaska.

In the privacy of correspondence with Neva, Egan could crow a little about his success in Fairbanks but then went on to assure his wife that their agreement about his future plans was still foremost in his mind:

> I have no ambitions whatsoever on that score and am perfectly ready to drop out of politics and give my thoughts to other things. It is a great compliment to have such a statement come from Snedden though. He is at heart a dyed in the wool Republican. Bartlett called me into the bathroom last night and told me about Snedden's conversation. Another thing that might interest you is that this woman, Mrs. Foster, who reports for the *Anchorage Daily News*, just stopped me on the stairs and said how thrilled she was at the job I have been doing in the chair. She said that wasn't just her opinion either, that it is the subject of conversation at dinners on the campus and in town where she has attended. She was amazed at how the Chairman could swing himself into any situation and resolve it without hard feeling and quickly make decisions acceptable to the whole body. Ha!... Have to go to KFAR and make a recording with Bob Bartlett at 4:30. Katie Alexander is having a dinner for several of the fellows at 6:30 and at 8 I'll meet with Bill O'Leary and Louie Ohman to go to the basketball game.

Years later, Katie Alexander Hurley recalled how they got together and sang at parties: "Bill Egan loved to sing and knew the words to all the old songs." Barrie White also remembered singing with Egan at parties that sometimes lasted all night.

Egan made sure that the convention sessions were open to the press but he did not welcome intervention by persons not officially part of the convention. Ernest Gruening, for instance, had a difficult time accepting that he was not an official part of the convention after giving his initial speech. After Gruening lost the governorship of Alaska when the national Republican administration appointed Frank Heintzleman in 1953, he spent much of his boundless energy sponsoring the cause of Alaska statehood throughout the nation and writing a bestselling history of Alaska's quest for self-government. He continued to stay in Fairbanks after his opening speech, receiving there news that his younger son, Peter, had committed suicide in Australia.

In a December 9, 1955, letter to his good friend Bob Bartlett, Egan expressed his frustration with Gruening:

> E.G. is still posing a problem. We had quite a time for a while. Vic Rivers and a very few more were insisting that he be put on the Convention payroll. Finally had to put Vic in his place in no uncertain terms. At the Patty dinner I was sitting alongside Bill Snedden. He leaned over and asked me what we were going to do about Gruening—to which yours truly pretended surprise. To Snedden I expressed the hope he was only going to be here only for the Convocation and a few days. Snedden then told me that wasn't so. Ha! He also told me about mentioning the matter to you, etc. When Bob Atwood came I had him come up and talked of the E.G. problem for about an hour. His possible solution was to put E.G. on the Statehood Committee payroll for a limited time and get him to do his work in a room at the Anchorage Hotel. E.G. is on the payroll but has not gone to Anchorage. Had a letter from Atwood today in which he mentioned that he had talked like a Dutch Uncle to E.G. E.G. is doing his work in an office at some other point on the campus but makes his regular appearance at Convention Hall. … In a way it is a terrible thing to write such things about such a man, but you'll understand.

Egan felt that he could discuss his irritation with Gruening's interference in the convention proceedings with Bartlett because Bartlett had used him as a confidant when Gruening, as Alaska's governor, interfered, uninvited, with proceedings in Washington, D.C.

In the same letter, Egan made the following comments to Bartlett regarding his own future plans:

> You know, Bob, it is actually going to be a great relief to me to be out of the candidate field. Neva thinks I am crazy, and I probably am. ... You are, in a way, fortunate, away from almost daily contact with certain <u>insincere party</u> people. You are where you are, too—in <u>spite</u> of them, rather than <u>because</u> of them. ... Bob, I'm very happy and proud of the honor that has been bestowed upon me on my last time around. Am only praying that I am able to do a fair enough job that you and other friends won't ever regret that I am in the chair.

Bartlett was still reluctant to accept Egan's decision to quit politics. He responded by letter on December 14:

> Before commenting on any other thing—and there will probably be comments on many other things—let me try to emphasize here what I said to you on a couple of occasions in Fairbanks. If it is essential to your business, positively and absolutely essential, that you remain out of political life for a time then I won't say another word. But if that is not the case then I am going to say many in an effort to get you to change you decision. Alaska simply cannot afford to lose you. I mean that very honestly and sincerely. Granted that you have no intention at all of staying out of public life for the long pull, yet the fact is that when a flood is in progress there cannot be permitted any shattering of the dike. And it will be shattered to a degree if you remove yourself. Everything was so

unsatisfactory at Fairbanks in that everyone was so busy that I more than ever regret now our lack of opportunity for a talk lasting sufficiently long so we could go to the bottom of this and plenty of other things too. Certainly if you decide to change your mind there would be no bad repercussions on account of the statement which came out of Valdez. How does Neva look at it? Does she want you out? After long experience, you and I know that the attitudes of our women are pretty darn important in our final decisions.

Egan had an opportunity to discuss the situation with Neva when he returned to Valdez during the convention recess for the Christmas and New Years holidays. Neva and 8-year-old Dennis returned to Fairbanks with him after the break. Most of the preliminary drafts had been written before the recess and the delegates had a chance to discuss them with their constituents. Upon return to the convention, committee chairmen read proposed articles to the delegates and answered their questions. After an article had had its second reading, the president referred it to the Enrollment and Engrossment Committee, which made sure that all amendments made in the second reading were incorporated in the original committee proposal. Finally, each proposed article was referred to the Style and Drafting Committee, which made sure it conformed with basic drafting guidelines, including present tense, simplicity, brevity, and uniformity of expression. The National Municipal League later termed the finished 14,400-word document "one of the best state constitutions ever written."

The proposed constitution was flexible enough to allow for changes that the future might bring and respected the equal rights and dignity of all Alaskans. The document called for a legislature consisting of 20 senators, elected to four-year terms, and 40 representatives serving two-year terms. An integrated state administration would be headed by a strong governor, who would appoint the attorney general and department commissioners. The governor would be elected for a four-year term and be eligible to succeed himself once. A unified court system was provided for, in which judges would be selected by the governor on nomination by a judicial council composed of representatives of the bar and the lay public. The decision to give the governor this much power was a reaction to the fragmentation of Alaska's territorial government. Since Alaska had no county structure, local government was placed in boroughs and cities. After extended debate on the name to be given to regional government, the term "borough" was selected instead of the more common "county". Local government powers were invested in boroughs and cities to avoid the proliferation of overlapping jurisdictions common in the United States. Alaska's natural resources were to be developed, whenever possible, for sustained yield, and the state government retained residual ownership in all state lands and their natural wealth for the benefit of all citizens. Initiative and referendum enabled Alaskans to enact laws and reject acts by the legislature. All elected officials, except judicial officers, were made subject to recall. Article V set the voting age at nineteen, provided the voter could read English. Amendments to the constitution, as provided for by Article XIII, could be added if approved by a two-thirds vote in each house of the legislature, and subsequently in a statewide election. Every ten years the question of whether to call a constitutional convention would be automatically placed on the ballot.

Egan was willing to defer action on several issues that might have caused sufficient sectional dissent to derail the convention. After considerable discussion on mechanisms to select the state capital, Section 20 of Article XV, Schedule of Transitional Measures, stated that, at least for the present, the capital would remain in Juneau. Although some delegates from Southcentral Alaska were anxious to have the capital located in an area more accessible to the majority of the population, they conceded the necessity of having a place designated as the capital should statehood be granted. Native land ownership was another potentially contentious issue that delegates were unwilling to consider. Native land claims were not a major

Convention President William A. Egan addressing delegates and public prior to signing the constitution on February 5, 1956.—MCC#25668, Steve McCutcheon Collection, AMHA.

concern at the time in Alaska although "Muktuk" Marston, who had spent time in rural Alaska organizing the National Guard during World War II, raised the issue, feeling that some means should be provided through which Natives could establish ownership of their land. Most of the delegates, however, felt that Native lands were a federal rather than a state problem.

All the delegates looked forward to signing the finished document except Ralph Robertson from Juneau who mailed his resignation to President Egan on February 3, 1956. He had several objections, including apportionment and an ordinance abolishing fish traps. He had attended the convention primarily to fight for the designation of Juneau as the capital of the future state. Signing of the constitution

Convention President William A. Egan was the first delegate to sign the constitution.—MCC#003, Steve McCutcheon Collection, AMHA.

took place before about 1,000 spectators in the University of Alaska gymnasium following the reading of a laudatory telegram from Delegate Bartlett and a brief address by Alaska Governor Heintzleman. As the delegates' names were called, they stepped forward one by one, paused and sat down long enough to sign the document. President Egan signed first and Secretary Stewart signed last.

Reverend Roland Armstrong, a delegate from Sitka, gave a benediction in which he referred to Egan: "We thank Thee for him. We thank Thee for his wisdom; it has been wisdom from above. We cherish his undaunted courage, the courage he has displayed before us as

Constitutional convention officers, First Vice President Frank Peratrovich, the only Alaska Native delegate, President William A. Egan, and Second Vice President Ralph Rivers, bow during benediction.—MCC#007, Steve Mc-Cutcheon Collection, AMHA.

delegates. We thank Thee for him." Following the prayer, President Egan gave a major address devoted to state-hood. He reviewed Alaska history from the time of pur-chase to the present, rebutting each argument that had been presented against statehood. He stressed that Alaska was ready for statehood and had the resources to support it. He finished with an expression of his commitment to Alaska: "We love our great United States of America, and our hearts belong to our great Territory of Alaska, and we will never have a true peace of mind until we are taken in full membership as one of the great states of the Union." The singing of *Alaska's Flag* ended the signing ceremony.

The delegates reconvened in a plenary session to sign additional copies of the constitution, take care of administrative arrangements, initiate actions toward ratification,

Convention President William A. Egan ducks behind the portrait presented him by the delegates. Michael J. Walsh and Ada B. Wien standing. Frank Peratrovich seated.— MCC#001, Steve McCutcheon Collection, AMHA.

and express thanks to various groups and individuals. Ada Wien of Fairbanks read the conventions final resolution:

> WHEREAS for seventy-five Convention days, the Honorable William A. Egan has served as presiding officer; and WHEREAS in this capacity he has demonstrated to

all his parliamentary skill, his unwavering fairness, his personal friendliness, and his untiring devotion to duty; and WHEREAS the delegates and officers of the Convention desire to express their gratitude for his outstanding leadership, in a form that will endure along with their admiration, and in form that will enable them to indicate their gratitude to his charming wife and son, that the Honorable William A. Egan, President of the Alaska Constitutional Convention of 1955, be asked to accept, as a token of our thanks, admiration, and affection, a portrait of himself, painted by the distinguished artist Christian von Schaedau on commission from the delegates, and that a copy of this resolution properly inscribed be presented to our esteemed President Egan.

Delegate Barrie White's wife, Daphne, described the events that followed:

The picture had been placed on his desk. Bill is a short man so when he stood behind it, it was impossible to see anything but the top of his head. He kept trying to express his thanks and, being unable to control himself, would duck behind the picture. Finally someone started clapping and the applause built on itself and hung in the room.

After remarks by 82-year-old Delegate E.B. Collins, who had served in the First Alaska Territorial Legislature in 1913, Delegate Mildred Hermann moved that the convention adjourn, and asked the delegates to do so "in memory of two great Alaskans who pioneered the statehood movement—Judge James Wickersham and Judge Anthony J. Dimond." Dimond, who died in Anchorage in 1953, did not live to witness the role Bill Egan, was continuing to play in implementing the plan for Alaska statehood that he had described back in 1940.

ALASKA-TENNESSEE PLAN

Alaskans had now taken the first two steps toward achieving statehood that Delegate Anthony Dimond outlined back in 1940. A referendum on statehood had passed and an Alaska State constitution had been written. Ratification of the constitution by voters was the next step. Delegates to the constitutional convention added an additional ordinance for voters to consider—the Alaska-Tennessee Plan, whereby two prospective senators and a prospective representative would be elected and sent to Washington, D.C., as lobbyists for Alaska statehood.

This plan for promoting statehood was first used 160 years before by Tennessee. When denied statehood, Tennessee elected its congressional delegation and sent them to Washington, D.C., without waiting for an enabling act. The delegation did such an effective job of lobbying that Tennessee achieved statehood on June 1, 1796, 65 days after its arrival in Washington. Following Tennessee's example, six additional territories—Michigan, California, Oregon, Kansas, Iowa and Minnesota—elected senators and representatives to Congress before achieving statehood, thus hastening their admission to the union.

Impetus for using the Tennessee Plan came from George H. Lehleitner, a New Orleans businessman, who became an advocate for Hawaii statehood while stationed there during

World War II. Lehleitner attempted to persuade leaders of the Hawaiian statehood movement to adopt the Tennessee Plan, but they rejected it as being too aggressive. In the fall of 1955, Lehleitner traveled to Alaska to promote the Tennessee Plan. Encouraged by his trip, he drafted a proposal and sent copies to Alaska statehood supporters in Congress and received favorable comments. The Alaska Constitutional Convention welcomed Lehleitner as an "Honorary Ambassador

George Lehleitner presents his Alaska-Tennessee Plan proposal to the constitutional convention on February 1, 1956. Left to right, Democratic National Committeeman Alex Miller, Lehleitner, Convention President Egan, Republican National Committeeman Walter J. Hickel.— MCC#25585, Steve McCutcheon Collection, AMHA.

of Goodwill." Democratic National Committeeman Alex Miller and Republican National Committeeman Walter Hickel escorted him to the podium to present his plan. When a draft of the Alaska-Tennessee Plan ordinance came before the convention, all 53 delegates present voted to approve it.

Lehleitner's efforts were aided by an endorsement from Delegate Bartlett. Initially Bartlett was concerned about possible negative reactions in Congress to the Tennessee Plan, but after analyzing the situation, he decided that the outlook for Alaska statehood was so bleak at the time that a stimulating factor might help and probably would do no harm. Although statehood for both Hawaii and Alaska had been supported by the Truman administration, President Eisenhower resisted giving statehood to the entire territory of Alaska, ostensively because it might be difficult to defend. Furthermore, bills that linked Alaska and Hawaii statehood together had been sidelined, not withstanding the attraction of balancing the admission of Alaska, currently a Democratic stronghold, with Hawaii, whose government was Republican at that time.

Convention delegates decided to place both an ordinance approving the Alaska-Tennessee Plan and an ordinance abolishing fish traps, along with the ordinance ratifying the constitution before voters in the primary election on April 24, 1956. This primary would also nominate party slates for the territorial legislature, the congressional delegate, the attorney general, and the highway commissioner, along with the first presidential preference primary in Alaska history. Since the February 1 filing deadline for the primary occurred before the convention was over, it was not be possible for the Alaska-Tennessee Plan delegation to be elected at the same primary. Not wishing to delay implementation of the Alaska-Tennessee Plan, the delegates decided to have the upcoming Democratic and Republican conventions nominate their respective Alaska-Tennessee Plan candidates to be voted on in the 1956 general election.

After adjournment of the constitutional convention, President Egan appointed a committee to make recommendations to the Alaska Statehood Committee for pre-ratification actions, including distribution of 15,000 copies of the proposed state constitution and 100,000 copies of "A Report to the People of Alaska from the Alaska Constitutional Convention", prepared by consultant John Bebout to provide a summary and explanation of the constitution, the Alaska-Tennessee Plan, and the Fish Trap Ordinance.

Egan, who was not running for reelection as a territorial senator, helped supervise activities and planned to travel throughout the territory to explain the constitution and promote a favorable vote. Convention delegates contributed to his travel expenses since this campaigning went beyond the educational activities supported by the Alaska Statehood Committee.

While Egan was in Valdez he received a confidential letter, written on February 21, from Delegate Bartlett in which Bartlett informed him that, although people assumed that he and Ernest Gruening would be nominated as the Democratic candidates for Alaska-Tennessee Plan senators, he had decided not to agree to run.

> If the Tennessee Plan is to have a chance for success the three people who come down from Alaska must devote to it all their time, all their energies, all they have. They cannot engage in other activities and do justice to the jobs to which they have been elected. Very frankly, Bill, this job of delegate is becoming too big for one man. ... If I were elected as a Tennessee Plan senator and took one hour off each day to serve with my Tennessee Plan colleagues then I should be missing a vital hour of the day here in the Delegate's office. It simply can't be. Additionally, there is always the possibility that Alaska's legislative interests would be harmed if statehood foes here desired to criticize on the basis of my occupying two jobs. Additionally, there very understandably could

be a feeling on the part of Alaskans that I was becoming overly greedy. There are other reason too, but these will suffice. So I am not going to run. All of this leads up, Bill, to the real purpose of this letter. It is to suggest that you give most serious consideration to filing for the other Senate seat. You are ideally equipped. I'll let my presentation stand on the above sentence without any elaborations. You could be elected. The only reason I should not want you to run is if you have any substantial doubts as to whether the legislature will appropriate the necessary funds to give effectiveness to the Tennessee Plan. You will be burning your financial bridges behind you. If you come here a Senator, I should guess that your involvement in public office from now on will be constant. And that would be to Alaska's benefit.

Egan answered this letter on February 28:

My active politicking days were over, or so, perhaps, I thought—when the Convention adjourned. Your letter of February 21st sort of knocked me for a loop and has caused me great concern. Regardless of what my decision might be, the sincerity of the statements you made will be cherished forever. The fact that I know they are way too generous is of no real concern. The important thing about those remarks, to me, is that a man of Bob Bartlett's stature has so much confidence in Bill Egan. …There are many things I would have to consider before any decision as to whether it would be possible for me to be available for nomination as you suggested. In the meantime, Bob, please reconsider your own decision and hold your mind open. So far as I personally am concerned, as I said before—honor enough has come to me by the very suggestion by you that I might be qualified to seek such a position.

Support from convention delegates and political leaders like Delegate Bartlett went a long way towards convincing Egan that he was the kind of leader Alaskans were looking for.

Alaskans turned out in record numbers for the April 24 primary. The Alaska State Constitution was ratified 17,477 to 8,180. As anticipated, the Alaska-Tennessee Plan Ordinance did not fare as well but passed with 61 percent of the total territory vote, in spite of receiving only 44 percent of the votes in Southeastern Alaska. The Fish Trap Abolition Ordinance was by far the most popular, winning by a ratio of more than five to one. Bartlett easily won the Democratic nomination for delegate.

The delegates to the Democratic Convention, held in Anchorage in June, talked Egan into running for Alaska-Tennessee Plan senator along with Ernest Gruening and selected Ralph Rivers to run for representative. When Egan contacted Neva in Valdez, she replied: "You know, it's your decision. Whatever you decide is fine. But I am not staying here and running the store by myself. If you go to Washington, the family goes." Egan agreed and accepted the nomination to run against Republican Robert Atwood, the editor of the *Anchorage Times,* who chaired the Alaska Statehood Committee. All three Democratic candidates won the Alaska-Tennessee Plan positions in the 1956 general election. Atwood was perceived as an Anchorage booster and got very few votes in Southeastern Alaska. Gruening defeated John Butrovich, the Fairbanks state senator who was running for reelection to his Senate seat at the same time, and Rivers beat Republican Charles Burdick. Gruening might have preferred serving with Atwood because they were good friends, and he perceived an advantage to having a Alaska-Tennessee Plan senator from each party.

Bill and Neva Egan did not have much time to plan for their trip to Washington, D.C. Their days running a Valdez grocery store were over. Unfortunately the manager they hired did not work out well and they eventually were forced to sell the store. The loss of the store in Valdez continued to be a sensitive subject for Egan. Years later on December 3, 1966, after a *New York Times* reporter who had interviewed the Atwoods, wrote that Egan was neither "imaginative nor progressive" and that his grocery business had not been successful, Egan wrote Arthur Ochs Sulzberger, president and publisher of the *New York Times* from the Alaska governor's office:

> The *Anchorage Times* on November 28, 1966 carried a New York Times Service article on Alaska by Charlotte Curtis which I would hardly expect to find in a newspaper of prestige such as yours. ... Any citizen has the right, of course, to say that I am not "imaginative" nor "progressive," but the statement concerning my past business enterprise is totally inaccurate. ...Here are the facts concerning my grocery business. In 1946, I took over a business establishment in my hometown of Valdez, Alaska, which had failed. There was no stock left. What I purchased was the bare building. I borrowed considerable sums of money to get the business going. I made a profit in each and every year I operated and paid federal and territorial income taxes every year. I constructed two new warehouses, installed modern equipment and otherwise upgraded the entire store. I built up a large stock inventory, had money in the bank, and did not owe one person a thin dime when I left Alaska for Washington in 1956 to serve as one of Alaska's elected provisional senators in the final drive for statehood. ... Perhaps this is what Miss Curtis meant in writing that I "was not successful" in business. ... But the implication of her statement is that I failed in business. I would hope, in the interest of fair play, that you will correct this damaging misstatement of fact.

Alaska-Tennessee Plan Senator William A. Egan, Representative Ralph Rivers, and wives prepare to leave the University of Alaska to drive to Washington, D.C. on December 9, 1956.—MCC#010, Steve McCutcheon Collection, AMHA.

ON TO WASHINGTON, D.C.

Alaskans prepared to launch an all out push for statehood after the election of the Alaska-Tennessee Plan delegation. A Fairbanks group persuaded "Senator" William Egan and "Representative" Ralph Rivers to drive from Fairbanks to Washington, D. C., stopping briefly in Tennessee and other states that had utilized the Tennessee Plan to achieve statehood. "Senator" Ernest Gruening, who had a home in Washington, D.C., declined to join the motorcade, but planned to rendezvous with the others at points along the way. To draw attention to the motorcade, statehood supporters arranged to have both the Egan and Rivers cars painted white and decorated with orange stickers proclaiming Alaska as the 49th state. The Egans agreed, but regretted having to ship their brand new red sedan to Fairbanks to have it painted.

On the afternoon of Sunday, December 9, the Egans and Rivers were honored in a farewell program at the University of Alaska. The following afternoon, with the thermometer registering 47 degrees below zero, they left Fairbanks in their white cars with the Alaska flag painted on each door. The battery in the Egans' car gave out before they reached Tok. They were forced to leave the car with all their belongings in it and drive to the 40-Mile Roadhouse with the Rivers. The temperature dropped further during the night. It was noon the next day before a tow truck could reach the car. Neva Egan recalled that the car bumped along on square tires when they towed it to the road-house where they stayed until the following day.

The rest of the trip over the Alaska Highway went well, but the delay caused the motorcade to miss its first meeting with Gruening, who took care of the publicity appointments. The Egans stopped in Kansas to celebrate Christmas with their 8-year-old son, Dennis, who had flown there to be with Neva's family rather than accompany his parents on the midwinter highway trip.

After visiting with the governor of Kansas, Egan and Rivers reached Tennessee in a snowstorm and joined Gruening for a reception at the governor's mansion. The Alaska-Tennessee Plan delegation was well received in all the states they visited, but Neva was not convinced that statehood for Alaska was a burning issue for the people they met. Finally, on December 31, three weeks after leaving Fairbanks, the weary travelers reached Washington, D.C. Delegate Bartlett welcomed them and informed them of preliminary work that was being done before Congress convened.

A group of Alaska statehood advocates had been in Washington for several weeks preparing for the congressional session. An unofficial committee, consisting of Delegate Bartlett, Dr. Ernest Bartley, a professor of political science at the University of Florida, who had been a consultant to the constitutional convention, and George Lehleitner had compiled dossiers on every member of Congress, containing information about their attitudes on statehood. Lehleitner also wrote a pamphlet describing the history of the Alaska-Tennessee Plan, which he sent to every Congressman and distributed widely to editors of newspapers and radio and television news programs.

Bill Snedden, editor of the *Fairbanks News-Miner,* was

a friend of Lehleitner and a supporter of the Alaska-Tennessee Plan. Snedden, an avid Republican who was anxious that Alaska achieve statehood during the Republican Eisenhower administration, contacted Secretary of Interior Frederick Seaton, who favored Alaska statehood. When Seaton asked Snedden to suggest someone to be a liaison between the Alaska-Tennessee Plan delegation and the Interior Department, Snedden recommended young Ted Stevens, who had recently left Fairbanks to take a position as legislative counsel for the Interior Department in Washington, D.C. Stevens was able to facilitate communications between visiting Alaska Republicans, such as Robert Atwood, Mike Stepovitch and Walter Hickel, and the Eisenhower administration. With the help of Atwood's daughter, Marilyn, Snedden and Stevens compiled information on congressmen for their own use. Snedden took a room at the Hotel Washington and stayed in Washington while the Legislature was in session. Snedden wrote editorials favoring Alaska statehood, capitalizing on his friendship with editors of newspapers and magazines throughout the country to popularize the cause. Since television was still in its infancy, newspapers were the primary mechanism through which to mobilize nationwide attention.

On January 14, 1957, Senator Spassard L. Holland of Florida read a memorial on the Senate floor asking Congress to "seat the duly-elected representatives and … enact legislation enabling the admission of Alaska to the Union of States." Senator Holland introduced the Alaska delegation, which was seated in the diplomatic gallery with their families. The senators greeted Gruening, Egan and Rivers with applause. The Senate did not vote to seat the Alaska-Tennessee Plan delegation officially, but Gruening, Egan, and Rivers were free act as lobbyists under the direction of Delegate Bartlett. Although Bartlett was not a strong supporter of the Alaska-Tennessee Plan, he did his best to help his fellow Alaskans in a productive manner. Most of the meetings took place in Bartlett's office, resulting in extra work and distraction for him and his staff which had other legislation to consider.

Egan, Gruening and Rivers spent most of their time talking directly with individual congressmen and their legislative aides. Egan gave Rivers considerable help in con-

Alaska Delegate to Congress E.L. (Bob) Bartlett with staff, Mary Lee Council and Margery Gadding Smith, in his Washington, D.C., office where the Alaska-Tennessee Plan delegates held many of their meetings.—MCC#018, Steve McCutcheon Collection, AMHA.

tacting almost 400 members of the House, where the statehood vote was considered to be most crucial. Egan's photographic memory was invaluable. According to Neva, Rivers often had to rely upon him to identify the individual representatives. In retrospect, Ted Stevens recalls that Egan was the most effective of the Alaska-Tennessee Plan delegation, particularly in his dealings with the House members. Gruening was too partisan a Democrat to deal effectively with some Senate Republicans. Bartlett and Egan were not viewed by congressional colleagues as being as partisan as Gruening, so they frequently were called upon to be peacemakers. Statehood was not a partisan issue—some members of each party favored it while others opposed it.

Office space and staff support presented a problem for the Alaska-Tennessee Plan delegation. They were hesitant to rent an office until the territorial Legislature provided funds. When a Alaska-Tennessee Plan office was finally established it was crowded. The one secretary was unable to serve all three delegates, so Rivers used his wife as his secretary in one corner of the downtown office. Rather than compete with Gruening for secretarial service, Egan set up an office in his Cleveland Park home. Gruening entertained lavishly in his Washington home and Rivers frequently went dancing socially, but Washington social life was a new experience for the Egans and their young son after many years in a small Alaska town. Furthermore, Egan was financially responsible for the money allocated by the territorial Legislature for the Alaska-Tennessee Plan delegates. Neva Egan recalled that her husband was reluctant to spend much on entertainment because he wanted to save enough to fund a statewide election should statehood be achieved.

In July of 1957, House Speaker Sam Rayburn, hitherto a foe of Alaska statehood, changed his mind. Statehood supporter Leo O'Brien of New York predicted that the Speaker's support would add at least 20 votes for the Statehood Bill should it be placed before the House. Speaker Rayburn recommended that consideration of the bill be deferred until 1958 rather than attempt to rush it through in the final days of the 1957 session. In the meantime, Delegate Jack Burns from Hawaii - a close friend of the Egans - decided that statehood for Alaska and Hawaii should not be combined in the same bill as they had been previously, since each territory had statehood opponents who combined to oppose previous legislation that combined the two territories. With Alaska gaining momentum, Burns threw his support to the Alaska Bill, assuming that, should Alaska achieve statehood, Hawaii would soon follow.

After Congress reconvened in January 1958, President Eisenhower stated his support of Alaska statehood for the first time, although he still advocated considering Alaska and Hawaii together. Delegate Burns stated firmly that nothing should interfere with consideration of Alaska and promised to remove the Hawaii Bill if necessary to assure the success of Alaska. This courageous move on the part of the Hawaii delegate, in the face of severe criticism from his constituents, was pivotal to the success of the Alaska Bill since some southern representatives opposed statehood for Hawaii because of its multiracial population.

During the spring of 1958, the Alaska Statehood Committee urged Alaskans to publicize the drive for statehood by writing friends and relatives in the states. Snedden continued to provide editorials to small town newspapers throughout the country. Both Alaska and Hawaii were featured on popular television programs, such as Edward R. Murrow's "See It Now." Ernest Gruening attributed nationwide sympathy for the Alaska cause to the publication of Edna Ferber's novel *Ice Palace* in May.

After a series of procedural manipulations, the debate on Alaska statehood opened in the House of Representatives in late May. Delaying tactics from statehood opponents, such as John R. Pillion of New York, criticized the tactics Alaska was using. Questioning the propriety of a territorial government using public funds to promote a political initiative, he deemed the election by Alaska of three Alaska-Tennessee Plan congressmen a presumptuous attempt to coerce Congress.

The House accepted an amendment by Representative William Dawson to reduce the land grant to the new state from 182,800,000 to 102,550,000 acres and, on May 28, rejected several attempts to postpone the final roll call. Representative Leo O'Brien of New York, who was promoting the bill in the House, still didn't think it would pass and had already packed his bags to go back to Albany. Neva Egan was more optimistic as she sat in the gallery rubbing her good luck ivory billiken.

> We knew it was do or die that night. … Bill had taken our car in to be serviced, because he knew this was it, we were going home no matter what. It was either going to pass or it was dead for another few years. … I had called Dennis to come down so he would be in the Gallery. … Just at the last minute Bill walked in, so he was there. When he was driving back to the Capitol in our car he decided to take a turn and go around in front of Union Station. He saw Leo O'Brien standing there with his bag waiting for a cab, so he stopped and picked Leo up. … Leo would have missed it if Bill hadn't picked him up at the railway station.

The roll-call vote was 210 to 166 in favor of statehood for Alaska, and the House sent the amended Alaska Statehood Bill to the Senate for action. The delighted Alaskans, Republicans and Democrats alike, convened in the Senate chapel. Following their prayers, Neva sang *Alaska's Flag*, impressing the group with her singing voice and her knowledge of the words.

Back in 1950, an Alaska statehood bill died in the Senate after passage by the House, but this time the Alaska-

Tennessee Plan delegation was confident that they had the necessary votes in the Senate to approve Alaska statehood providing differences between the Senate and House bills could be reconciled. To Delegate Bartlett's relief, Senator Henry "Scoop" Jackson of Washington, who was promoting the Alaska Statehood Bill in the Senate, agreed to accept the House bill. The Senate debated the bill throughout the month of June with several southern senators attempting, unsuccessfully, to make amendments. The statehood opponents finally gave up on June 30, 1958, and the Alaska Statehood Bill passed with 64 senators in favor and 20 opposed.

After President Eisenhower signed the Alaska Statehood Bill in private on July 7, Alaskans prepared to elect two real senators, a representative, and their own governor. Bill Egan had succeeded in saving enough money from the territorial appropriation to hold a primary election on August 26 to approve immediate admission of Alaska to the Union and determine the Republican and Democratic slates for the November general election. Egan faced an agonizing decision about which office to file for. Ernest Gruening immediately filed for a Senate seat and Ralph Rivers for the House of Representatives, leaving Bartlett and Egan to make their decisions. Bartlett hesitated and Egan, assuming that Bartlett would want to be Alaska's first governor, filed for Senate on July 7. During an interview with Claus Naske in 1977, Egan stated that he had filed for Senate at Bartlett's suggestion. Although Egan assumed that Bartlett wanted the governorship, the delegate may have actually wanted Egan to defeat Gruening for one of the Senate seats so Bartlett would have him instead of Gruening as a Senate colleague.

Egan was receiving advise from various sources. John Bebout, assistant director of the National Municipal

League, who had been a consultant at the constitutional convention, talked with Neva Egan.

> He called from New York and wanted to talk to Bill. Well, Bill wasn't home—he was down still delivering things to the senators. I think he was taking around Alaska newspapers telling about how we'd finally won it, and how it was the victory was covered in Alaska. He said, "What's Bill going to run for?" Since Bill wasn't there, he decided to talk to me instead. I said, "Well, he's filed for the Senate," and he replied, "Oh, I'm sorry to hear that. ... I had so hoped he'd file for governor. The power is in that first governor. Anyone can be governor after that, but the first governor needs so badly to be an honest man and to get that State off to a good start, ... From what I've seen, the only ones that I would trust to be the first governor are Bill Egan and Bob Bartlett. Bill would be first choice because he's been on the local scene more lately."

Vide Bartlett, who was also interviewed by Claus Naske in 1977 during the preparation for his biography of Bartlett, commented on the problem that her husband and Egan were having in deciding which office to run for. She expressed her opinion that the governorship was the hardest job of them all and that nobody was as well prepared to run for the governorship as Egan because he lived in the country, served in the legislature, and was an author of the constitution that puts the governor as the central figure with nobody as powerful as the governor. She went on to say that, although her husband considered it the most important job, he was a legislator rather than an administrator.

Bartlett finally announced his decision to file for one of the Senate seats. The Senate seats were designated individually so that Egan would be facing Gruening in the primary election. In the 1977 interview with Naske, Egan stated: "There is no question in my mind that certain people were trying to do Ernest in and felt the best way was for me to lock horns with Ernest head on." Egan felt he was popular enough in Alaska to win the election but did not want to stand in the way of the aging Gruening, whose lifeline desire was to serve in the Senate. Furthermore the Egans were anxious to leave Washington, D.C. When he realized that Bartlett did not want to be governor of Alaska, Egan gladly changed his mind and filed for the governorship. Years later in 1975, Dorothy Gruening wrote Egan a note saying that she wanted to tell him again how much Ernest and she were grateful that Egan pulled out of the Senate race.

The August primary election confirmed Alaska's immediate admission to the Union with a vote of 40,421 in favor to only 7,766 opposed. The Democratic primary nominated Bartlett to run for senior senator, Gruening for junior senator, Rivers for representative, Egan for governor, and Bartlett's good friend, Hugh Wade, for secretary of state. Egan still had to win the November general election in which he faced his friend state Senator John Butrovich from Fairbanks. During the campaign Egan was saddened by editorials critical of the Alaska-Tennessee Plan delegation in the *Fairbanks News-Miner*. Editor Snedden probably hoped to sway voters to support the Republican ticket. Alaskans, however, registered their satisfaction with the Alaska-Tennessee Plan delegation by electing the Democratic ticket.

William A. Egan campaigning for the Alaska governorship in the Homer public school on November 11, 1958—MCC#9309, Steve McCutcheon Collection, AMHA.

A TOUGH FIRST YEAR AS GOVERNOR

While awaiting returns from the election, Robert Atwood, Egan's former Republican rival, editorialized in the *Anchorage Times* on the challenges facing the new governor:

> The man who wins the governorship gets our sympathy. He will carry the biggest responsibility in establishing the new state government. He must appoint the key men who will operate the agencies of the executive branch. He must appoint the judges of the new state court system. … The pitfalls for the governor are so numerous that it is frightening. So much depends upon him that a major portion of the fate of the state rests in his hands. … The new governor must approach the job with the ambition to serve all Alaskans. He is to be the governor for all and not just those of the party that gave him the majority vote. … There is no pat formula to follow in the shaping of the new state. Policies, rules and procedures must be made that will affect the future as much as the present generation.

Egan immediately planned to meet these challenges after defeating Butrovich by nearly a three-to-one majority. From his home in Valdez, he announced that he would begin work as Alaska's governor-elect in Juneau on December 8 although no provisions had as yet been made for compensating the new governor. In a telegram to

Acting Territorial Governor Waino Hendrickson, he asked each territorial department head to submit appropriation requests so that he could work on the draft of an appropriation bill to submit to the First State Legislature in January. When he arrived in Juneau, Egan gave an address at the Baranof Hotel and made temporary housing arrangements until the Egan family could move into the governor's mansion after the inauguration. Egan then contacted Burke Riley, who had served with him during the constitutional convention, and John Rader, the young Anchorage lawyer who had been his campaign manager, to meet him in Juneau and help him make preparations for assuming the governorship. Although Hugh Wade, the newly-elected secretary of state, lived in Juneau, both Riley and Rader indicated that he did not take an active part in this advance planning.

Upon arriving in Juneau, Rader found that no provisions had been made for office space or clerical support. That the territorial officials had little regard for Egan seemed obvious to him. Rader's spent time studying congressional hearings on the Alaska Statehood Bill to get an understanding of the legislative intent. He also studied the state constitution, relying heavily on Egan's memory because the proceedings had not as yet been transcribed. Egan discussed some possible administrative appointments with Riley and Rader, but no decisions could be made until the Legislature decided on departmental structure. The constitution did not create specific executive departments, merely limiting them to no more than twenty. A summary prepared by Public Administrative Services, the advisory group at the constitutional convention, recommended 11 executive departments: Health and Welfare, Education, Administration, Law, Revenue, Labor and Commerce, Local Affairs, Military Affairs, Natural Resources, Public Safety, and Public Works.

Since the lack of office space was delaying his work, Egan decided to get a medical checkup and entered the Juneau hospital on December 9 for a hemorrhoidectomy. His recovery from this minor surgery was slow and by the time he was sworn in as governor on January 3, 1959, he had lost weight and was visibly jaundiced. Immediately after the ceremony, Egan was admitted to St. Ann's Hospital where he underwent sur-

Alaska Governor-elect William A. Egan given the oath of office by Judge Raymond J. Kelly on January 3, 1959. Note the deterioration in his physical condition as compared to the picture taken six weeks before.—Photo courtesy of Gerald Bowkett.

gery for removal of the gall bladder and a gall stone in the common bile duct.

Mindful of the overwhelming vote on the Fish Trap Ordi-

115

nance, Egan's first action as governor was to abolish fish traps in Alaska. He also announced the appointment of Burke Riley of Haines as executive assistant, Lillian Mill as state treasurer to succeed Hugh Wade, and John Rader as a special assistant. An article in the *Daily Alaska Empire* speculated that Rader would be appointed attorney general. However, the Republican Territorial Attorney General J. Gerald Williams announced that he had no intention of resigning since he had been elected for a term that would not expire for two more years. Rader and Riley visited Egan several times in the hospital, but Egan was too sick to do much. They frequently had to act according to their own best judgment since Secretary of State Wade was not aware of Egan's plans and was reluctant to make decisions on his own while Egan was still the official governor. Although Egan was initially reported to be recovering well, the inauguration was postponed until February 7.

Egan's condition began to deteriorate seriously around January 13 when he complained of discomfort and abdominal distention. On January 19, Wade was appointed acting governor and Egan was evacuated by air to Virginia Mason Hospital in Seattle where he underwent emergency surgery. Although initially given only a 50 percent chance for recovery from peritonitis caused by leakage of bile into the abdominal cavity, Egan rallied after surgery, which drained three to four quarts of accumulated bile, but continued to be desperately ill. Neva, who accompanied her husband to Seattle, described his condition in a January 30 letter to Burke Riley:

> I want you to know that the doctor feels Bill will be out here about two months more, at the most. He will have to have another gall stone removed when he has been built up enough - possibly in a month. It is a stone they couldn't remove in Juneau, nor could they remove it here, because of the time involved. ... I'm sure that part of the depressed feeling comes from worrying about not being on the job. ... Everyday he

makes more progress, but he is so terribly weak that it worries him, I know. You can't imagine how thin he is. He had his last IV today and is now taking all his food by mouth... He will be out of the hospital for a time between operations, so that will help some. … He reads the paper every day and I'm sure will be up to phone conversations in a week or two.

As Egan's condition improved, Riley visited him several times in Seattle.

The First State Legislature convened on January 26, 1959, and elected William E. Beltz, an Inupiat Eskimo from Unalakeet, president of the Senate and Fairbanks attorney Warren A. Taylor speaker of the House of Representatives. Three days after the session began, Acting Governor Wade met with majority and minority leaders to discuss prompt attention to the reorganization of the executive branch, which would involve reconciling differences between the recommendations of the PAS report and the Legislative Council plan calling for 13 major state departments. Frequent discussions related to whether heads of the Education and Fish and Game departments should be appointed by the governor or by their respective commissions. The constitution allowed a board or commission to be head of these particular departments, having in mind their regionalized constituencies. The chief executive of these departments was subject to gubernatorial approval, but the constitution left open who was to be the appointing authority. Prompt action was also needed to determine the salaries for the governor, the new department commissioners and the legislators. Rader assumed his seat in the House of Representatives and was appointed head of the House Committee on State Affairs, placing him in position to act as liaison between the Legislature and the executive branch.

Senator Bartlett visited Egan in the Seattle hospital in the middle of February and reported that he was still a very sick man in no condition to see many people or transact business. Egan had recovered sufficiently by February 27 to be discharged from the hospital and continue convalescing for an additional six weeks in a Seattle apartment. Dennis Egan, who was still attending school in Juneau, flew to Seattle in early March to celebrate his 12th birthday with his mother and father. Egan attended the christening of a Standard Oil tanker with Neva on April 1, and served as marshal of the Puyallup Valley daffodil parade the following week. On April 12, the Juneau paper announced that the governor would visit Juneau if his doctors approved.

On April 4, Acting Governor Wade signed the Reorganization Bill, which affirmed the strong executive government provided for in the constitution, leaving the governor to appoint commissioners for 12 established departments, each also to serve in the governor's cabinet. Wade immediately announced the appointment of Floyd Guertin, a former Juneau airline executive approved by Egan, as commissioner of administration to be confirmed by the Legislature. Wade made no other appointments until Governor Egan returned to Juneau on April 13.

In a final joint session, the Legislature unanimously approved Egan's choices for four additional cabinet-level appointments. Egan appointed John Rader as Alaska's first state attorney general, squeezing out Territorial Attorney General Williams. Egan retained Territorial Commissioner Phil Holdsworth of Juneau, as commissioner of natural resources and appointed Richard A. Downing of Fairbanks as commissioner of public works and highways and Lewis Dischner, a Teamster Union official from Fairbanks, as commissioner of labor.

Egan officially reassumed the governorship on Monday, April 20. In a lengthy interview with the *Daily Alaska*

Empire, he praised the Legislature for completing the session in 81 days. "Honestly, the fact that they came up with a balanced budget, while providing the necessary funds for health, welfare, education and the possibility of taking over court system and fisheries, is amazing. And don't forget the state reorganization bill. When I left here people were talking about a six month session and a fall session. There also were no new tax increases passed." Egan also sent a letter of commendation to Secretary of State Wade expressing his abiding appreciation for devoted performance of duties and functions during his absence. He then began considering the legislative bills awaiting his signature to become law.

Although the constitution gave Egan the power to make line item vetoes, he signed most of the bills passed by the Legislature, including an appropriation for a mental hospital in Valdez, a Workmen's Compensation Insurance Act, a Blue Sky Act to regulate and control the sale of securities in the state, and bills creating magistrates courts and a State Public Service Commission. He also signed the 31 and 1/3 million dollar Appropriation Bill into law without change and signed bills relating to the classification and powers of cities. Egan's only vetoes were registered on the controversial Employment Security Bill and a measure that would have outlawed the duplication of electrical transmission lines. Before leaving Juneau on May 20 to have his final surgery in Seattle, Egan announced cabinet appointments of Paul Winsor of Anchorage to head the Department of Health and Welfare and Peter Gatz of Fairbanks to be commissioner of revenue.

Immediately upon his return to Alaska on June 13 to resume his gubernatorial duties, Egan was forced to deal with the first of several conflicts in the fishing industry. Native fishermen in three Southeastern villages, Metlakatla, Kake and Angoon announced that they planned to operate their 11 fish traps in spite of state law outlawing traps. Leaders of these villages maintained that rights granted the Natives by the federal government provided authority for continuous use of the traps. Even though the federal government specifically authorized the villages to operate these traps, Governor Egan was adamant that there be no exceptions to the prohibition.

On his way back from Seattle, Egan arranged meetings with tribal leaders in all three villages to discuss the problem before the first trap fishing was scheduled to begin on June 24. With no resolution in sight, two boats from the special state anti-fish-trap police force, a special unit assigned to regulate fish traps, began patrolling Kake and Angoon waters. The chief enforcement officer of the Alaska Department of Fish and Game reported that they were watching fishermen readying the traps for operation. Legal entanglements began on June 17 with the arrest of Ernest Williams, president of the Organized Village of Kake. The Interior Department in Washington then authorized use of village funds for Kake and Angoon to employ legal counsel. R.J. Jernberg, the Ketchikan lawyer hired by the villages, planned to file an injunction in civil court forbidding state enforcement of the ban on fish traps. A United States attorney was designated to defend Williams in the criminal case. Attorney General Rader and Special Fisheries Counsel James Fitzgerald, former Anchorage city attorney, would represent the state in both civil and criminal cases. Native opinion was divided on the case with the Alaska Native Brotherhood backing Egan in the state's fight against fish traps. An ANB executive explained that the conflict was between the state and the Indian Reorganization Act administration of the Bureau of Indian Affairs, which was financing the fishing and canning operations in Kake and Angoon. The conflict was temporarily resolved on July 12 when United States Supreme Court Justice William J. Brennan Jr. granted a preliminary injunction to prevent Alaska from halting the operation of the Native fish traps. The traps were allowed to fish and the state was given until August 20 to file objections. According to the Alaska Statehood Act, the Interior Department retained responsibility for administering wildlife resources in the state until January 1, 1960. Once the state assumed this responsibility, the Alaska Supreme Court would have jurisdiction in the case.

Prompt establishment of a state Supreme Court was a priority for the new Egan administration and Egan announced appointments of the three justices authorized by the constitution at a special news conference at the end of July. Egan made his selections from names submitted by the six-man Judicial Counsel charged with the job of presenting names to the governor for judicial appointments. The governor named Anchorage lawyer Buell A. Nesbitt to be chief justice and U.S. District Judge Walter J. Hodge from Nome and John H. Dimond, a Juneau attorney, to associate justice positions. Egan was especially pleased to nominate Dimond, his boyhood friend and son of former Delegate Anthony J. Dimond to a position on the state's highest court. Dimond and Egan continued to be close friends, frequently meeting in Egan's office early in the morning before others arrived at work.

Under provisions of the Alaska Statehood Act, the four regional federal territorial district courts would be replaced within two years by a single federal court for the District of Alaska. The state Legislature had already authorized eight superior court judges and a system of local magistrates. As required by the constitution, Chief Justice Nesbitt joined the Judicial Council to consider names to be submitted to the governor for superior court appointments.

Alaska's continued subservience to the federal government was displayed in several instances involving Alaska lands, as well as in the fish trap case. Governor Egan objected to the proposed withdrawal of 9 million acres in northeast Alaska for an Arctic Wildlife Refuge, but his plea for a statewide referendum on the withdrawal failed to influence Eisenhower's Interior Secretary Fred Seaton. Then, on August 17, the *Daily Alaska Empire* announced that President Eisenhower had vetoed a bill to raise the limit of oil and gas leases on federal land that a single company could hold in Alaska from 300,000 to 600,000 acres. Egan did not openly oppose the Project Chariot plan for an atomic blast in northwest Alaska, but urged the Atomic Energy Commission to provide funds for a state official to evaluate the safety of the project.

Improvement of transportation in Southeast Alaska was another priority consideration for the first Egan administration. Discussions with Canadian officials led to the designation of a potential transportation corridor up the Stikine River from Wrangell to the Cassiar Highway under construction in British Columbia. However, Southeastern Alaska communities favored a year-round ferry system from Prince Rupert in British Columbia to Haines as "the major highway through Southeast Alaska," to be supported by winter opening of the Haines Cutoff to the Alaska Highway.

As the end of Egan's first year as governor approached, he could look back on significant accomplishments in spite of a slow start, complicated by his illness. Reappointment of Brigadier General Thomas P. Carroll as state adjutant general in September and the appointment of California educator, Dr. Theodore Nerby, as commissioner of education completed Egan's cabinets selections. The Alaska Supreme Court was ready to begin holding sessions in early October, and Egan announced the appointment of eight superior court judges in November. James A. von der Heydt from Nome would serve in Juneau and Walter E. Walsh of Juneau in Ketchikan. Fairbanks residents Harry O. Arned and Everett W. Hepp would fill

Fairbanks positions and state Senator Hubert A. Gilbert would serve in Nome. The three Anchorage superior court judges would be state Senator J. Earl Cooper, Edward V. Davis, and James M. Fitzgerald, who had already served Egan as special counsel on fisheries and commissioner of public safety. The Republican state chairman complained that Egan had "packed the court" with Democratic lawyers, but Egan responded that the four federal judges in Alaska had all been Republicans and that, of the 17 potential nominees designated by the Judicial Council, only two were Republicans.

Alaska was preparing to take over the management of fish and game on January 1, 1960, as specified in the Alaska Statehood Act. As a result Alaska would take on some 25 new employees, who would shift over from federal fish and wildlife management to the payroll of the Alaska Department of Fish and Game. Regulations, drafted by the Fish and Game Board after hearings throughout the state, were designed to help rebuild depleted fisheries, long a sore point under federal administration.

Governor Egan commented on a new threat to state harmony when newsmen began asking him about a campaign that was starting in Anchorage to move the capital from Juneau. Egan replied that the constitution had placed the capital at Juneau and that it was too soon to consider a move, although studies regarding eventual capital location might be justified. On October 12, Egan spoke out more decisively, stating that the "chief accomplishment of this controversy has been to cause deep and wide sectional wounds at a time when all Alaskans must be united." He added: "I cannot encourage a move to devastate the economy of one of our cities - an action that would most certainly cause a permanent breach in our great state." Egan continued to foster statewide cooperation rather than sectionalism as he had while serving in the territorial legislature.

Agitation continued in Anchorage. Democratic Representative James Fisher was sponsoring an initiative to move the capital and local Anchorage developers were offering 50 acres of "good, high ground" for a new capital. Meanwhile, the city of Juneau disclosed plans to purchase an 18.7-acre plot for construction of new state buildings. On November 12, Secretary of State Wade challenged a request seeking voter enactment of a law to move Alaska's capital from Juneau, stating that the proposal was an attempt to amend the constitution by enactment of a law rather than by constitutional amendment. Wade referred the matter to Attorney General Rader and Rader answered with a 12-page legal opinion stating that Wade did not have the legal authority to deny certification of an initiative application because he thought it was an attempt to amend the constitution. The petition in question sought voter enactment of a law to move the capital from Juneau to the Cook Inlet - Railbelt area.

As the holidays approached, young Dennis Egan looked forward to his first Christmas "at home" in four years. In his Yuletide message, Governor Egan stated: "This year Alaskans received one of the most cherished gifts which can be bestowed upon man—the right of self-government as exemplified in full membership in our Union of States." Egan had much to be thankful for personally. After a life-threatening illness, he was finally enjoying good health with no future surgery to contemplate. A salary of $25,000 and lodging in the governor's mansion were compensations for losses the Egans had suffered in the sale of the Valdez grocery business. In spite of all the newsworthy accomplishments of the new state, Governor Egan's near fatal illness rated as Alaska's top news story in 1959 according to the Associated Press poll of newspaper editors.

SUMMARY OF THE EGAN GOVERNORSHIPS

In spite of time lost while recovering from his life-threatening illness, Egan completed the primary duties of Alaska's strong governor during his first year in office. With commissioners in charge of departments in the newly-organized executive branch and judges ready to take over judicial functions of the new state, Egan concentrated on other priorities. The people of Southeastern Alaska had shown their interest in a marine highway system to link semi-isolated communities and enhance tourism. Over protests from other regions of Alaska that the program was too large, the $18 million bond issue, proposed by Egan and approved by voters in 1960, enabled the purchase of three large ferries - *Malaspina*, *Matanuska*, and *Taku* - to serve Southeastern communities and the smaller *Tustumena* to provide ferry service to Southcentral ports like Valdez, Cordova, Homer, Seward and Kodiak. Shortly after they became operational in 1963, the three vessels serving Southeastern Alaska were carrying capacity loads of people and vehicles during the summer months, beginning the tourism industry that would become a mainstay of the Southeast economy in years to come.

With the advent of statehood, Alaska could issue general obligation bonds - a revenue source unavailable in territorial days. Egan used this mechanism to fund capital improvements such as roads, hospitals and airports. However, a $9 million bond issue for state office complexes in Anchorage and Fairbanks failed to get voter approval because some people were happy with a system that required the rental of privately-owned office space. Some voters opposed the building of state office buildings in Anchorage and Fairbanks because they considered it a move to forestall efforts to move the capital from Juneau. Although capital move initiatives twice failed to get voter approval over the ensuing twenty years, this divisive issue haunted Egan throughout his three terms as governor.

Selection of the 103 million acres allotted Alaska in the Statehood Bill was a major undertaking for the new state administration. Initially Egan, true to the fiscal conservatism engendered by his impoverished boyhood in small-town Alaska, was slow to obtain land for fear of incurring too much state expense related to selected land. Federal revenue sharing with the state was also based on the amount of federally retained land. However, he did heed the advise of Natural Resource Commissioner Phil Holdsworth and geologist Tom Marshall to select the North-Slope land at Prudhoe Bay where oil would soon be discovered. The federal government froze state land selections shortly thereafter pending settlement of aboriginal Native land claims.

Prior to statehood, cities, school districts and utility districts were all recognized forms of local government in Alaska. The state constitution provided that boroughs and cities should be the local providers of services such as planning, schools, and the levying of taxes. When some of the more populous parts of the state were reluctant to form these boroughs voluntarily, the Legislature passed a law mandating boroughs in reluctant areas with sufficient population such as Anchorage, Fairbanks, Matanuska-Susitna Valley, and Kenai Peninsula.

Fisheries continued to provide challenges for the new governor that thrust him into the field of international diplomacy. In the spring of 1962, a Japanese herring fleet was reported to be approaching Shelikof Strait, a body of water separating Kodiak Island from the Alaska Peninsula. Getting no response from the State Department when he asked for a warning to the Japanese, Egan mobilized the "Alaskan Navy." He manned the State Fish and Game Department's patrol boats with national guardsmen and state police officers and ordered them to intercept the invading fleet. Captain E. L. Mayfield of the Alaska State Police boarded a 65-foot herring catcher and ordered it into port on charges of "willfully and unlawfully operating a commercial fishing enterprise in Alaskan waters." United States Attorney General Robert F. Kennedy was soon on the telephone with Egan asking what on earth he thought he was doing. Egan responded, "I told you we would do something if you didn't act." Tokyo protested and the State Department stalled. After inconclusive hearings in Alaska State Courts, the Japanese withdrew from the disputed waters. Alaska's claim to the Shelikof Strait, if not confirmed, at least remained open.

When a dispute with Russian fishermen escalated in 1963, the State Department named Egan to a negotiating team. Egan's mission to Moscow was long remembered by his Russian hosts for his singing of all the verses of the ballad *Abdul Abulbul Amir*. The Russians signed a statement of agreement on general principles and promised to send negotiators to the United States to work out ways of avoiding future conflicts, specifying that the sessions be held in Juneau rather than Washington D.C. After two weeks of negotiations and reciprocal vodka and whiskey receptions - some on the Russians' ocean-going tug and others in the governor's mansion, the Russians agreed not to use nets where they might foul up American crab pots. Egan was proud of this resolution of problems dur-

Governor William A. Egan, center, with Secretary of State Hugh Wade, left, and Senator Ernest Gruening, right, on October 1, 1962.—MCC#002, Steve McCutcheon Collection, AMHA.

ing the height of the Cold War and stated: "It was the first occasion in which Soviets were willing to sit down with any fishing group in the world and talk over problems and work out a solution."

After assuring a second term by defeating former Alaska Territorial Governor Mike Stepovitch in the 1962 gubernatorial election, Egan demonstrated his willingness to take on American monopolies as well as foreign governments. In another unorthodox maneuver, he defied American salmon packers by inviting the Japanese to buy the entire catch of pink salmon in Prince William Sound. The Alaska Packers Association and the New England Fish Company of Seattle had said they would close their canneries unless Alaskan fishermen accepted a cut in price. The Japanese paid the higher price while Seattle and San Francisco processors screamed treason. Most Alaskan were delighted that local fishermen had been able to challenge the economic power of the canneries, although some old timers were uncomfortable with this arrangement with the recent deadly enemy and invader of their state.

The greatest challenge of Governor Egan's second term came on March 27, 1964 when an earthquake, rated 9.2 on the Richter Scale, shook Southcentral Alaska. The quake hit the Egans personally since the epicenter was close to Valdez. Their home, containing Egan's pre-governorship papers, was damaged, and 31 of his fellow Valdezians lost their lives when the city dock collapsed and a sunami swept through the town. Egan made an immediate aerial survey of the affected communities and, during the next two days, held a series of meetings with state officials to coordinate emergency measures and plan for the recovery effort. He decided that the state efforts had to be supplemented by massive federal assistance and, to support his case, compiled the State Earthquake Disaster Damage Report, which estimated loss of between $373 and $486 million (exclusive of federal property). The Legislature convened a few days later and authorized the $50 million in disaster bonds recommended by Egan.

Egan then assembled a party consisting of legislative leaders from both parties, representatives of labor and business, mayors of the affected cities, and key state officials to travel to Washington D.C. for consultation with the Reconstruction and Development Commission. On April 11, Egan addressed the state Legislature to review the

Earthquake damage assessment review at Elmendorf AFB on Easter Sunday morning, March 29, 1964. Left to right, Office of Emergency Planning Director Edward A. McDermott, Alaska Governor William A. Egan, Lt. General Raymond J. Reeves, Senator Ernest Gruening, Senator E.L. (Bob) Bartlett.—MCC#8576, Steve McCutcheon Collection, AMHA.

prospects for federal assistance: "Already several positive things have occurred. On Monday, Congress appropriated an initial fifty million dollars toward reconstruction projects. … The action came with unprecedented speed. Shortly thereafter the President proposed an extension of the Federal Transitional Grant Program and an appropriation of $22.5 million for this purpose. ... On my return to Washington on Monday, I will carry with me facts and figures citing why budget support items should be increased."

Governor Egan arranging for trailers in April 1964 to house Valdez residents who lost homes in the earthquake and tidal wave.—MCC#004, Steve McCutcheon Collection, AMHA.

The September 30, 1964 *Congressional Record* contained Senator Bartlett's assessment of the role Egan was playing in the post-earthquake reconstruction: "On the day following the creation of the Federal Reconstruction Commission, Alaska's Gov. William A. Egan—whose leadership has been remarkable in every way—established the Alaska Reconstruction and Development Planning Commission, which worked with the Federal Commission in the restoration of Alaska."

Although Bartlett registered this praise for Egan's leadership, the friendship between the two men cooled after Egan assumed the governorship. In the interview with historian Claus Naske prior to the publication of his biography of Bartlett, Egan speculated that Bartlett was reluctant to share the spotlight with others and resented that he was not consulted more frequently on matters that Egan was handling in Alaska. In his position as Alaska's strong governor, Egan was receiving nationwide publicity. The October 1965 issue of *Harper's Magazine* contained an article by Murray Morgan entitled "The Most Powerful Governor in the U.S.A." in which he reviewed Egan's small-town-Alaska roots and described his power as governor, including the confrontations with foreign governments over fishing rights. Bartlett, on the other hand, was faced with declining health, complicated by heavy smoking, and continued conflict with his Senate compatriot, Ernest Gruening. As the 1968 election approached, state Representative Mike Gravel, emboldened by Gruening's opposition to President Lyndon Johnson's Gulf of Tonkin resolution, challenged Gruening for Senate. Bartlett chose not to endorse Gruening and Gravel was elected. Bartlett's health continued to decline and he died in December 1968.

Egan was increasingly comfortable in his role as governor. His retentive memory was a major political asset and became legendary. He was able to greet many Alaskans by name and speak with them in a manner that demonstrated his interest in them and their families. During his frequent airplane trips, Egan made a practice of walking down the aisle to greet his fellow passengers. As the 1966 gubernatorial election approached, he was reluctant to retire from the political spotlight and leave Juneau. Although the Alaska State Constitution limited the governor to two successive terms, Egan filed again with the justification that his first term had not been a complete one because President Eisenhower did not sign the Statehood Bill until January 1959 instead of December 1958. Furthermore, Egan and his supporters reasoned

Governor Egan's home in Valdez was a victim of the 1964 tidal wave. Although the house appears to be intact, it suffered structural damage and flooding that destroyed records and pictures. The Egans did not feel the house was in good enough condition to be moved to the new Valdez townsite. After his defeat in the 1966 election, the Egans moved to Anchorage.—Photo courtesy of Gerald Bowkett.

that the four months spent in the Seattle hospital had further cut into his first term. This rational did not convince enough voters and Egan was narrowly defeated by Anchorage Republican hotel and construction entrepreneur, Walter J. Hickel, who ran an aggressive campaign. Hickel cut into the traditionally Democratic Alaska Native vote by advocating prompt settlement of their aboriginal land claims.

Since Egan's home in Valdez was destroyed, his family moved to Anchorage where he became a sales representative for Equitable Life Assurance. Alaska changed significantly during the four years that Egan was out of office as a result of the oil discovery at Prudhoe Bay. After two years as governor, Hickel accepted the post of secretary of interior in Richard Nixon's cabinet and turned the governorship over to Lieutenant Governor Keith Miller. The 1969 sale of North Slope oil leases enriched the Alaska treasury by $900 million, but development of oil wells was stalled by Native claims and the federal land freeze imposed by Interior Secretary Stuart Udall, Hickel's predecessor, that prevented construction of a pipeline to bring oil to tidewater. Egan felt he was capable of dealing with these issues and filed for governor to face Keith Miller in the 1970 election. This time Egan espoused the Native land claims issue, promising state participation while Miller considered the land claims strictly a federal issue. With the Native vote solidly behind him, Egan and his running-mate, Fairbanks Mayor "Red" Boucher, won easily.

Egan had always been cautious about offering oil and gas lands for competitive bid before knowing their true worth. He decried the North Slope lease sale because he felt some land should have been withheld until drilling actually began. Egan felt that control of Alaska oil would be the primary issue during his third term. He did not trust the oil industry and wanted to make sure that the state would receive maximum benefit from oil development. He used the public's mistrust of outside industry, resulting from the control that fishing and mining industries had in territorial days, to dampen the oil lobby and increase the share of oil revenue going to the state.

Since oil revenue depended on bringing the oil to market, the top priority for the state was to settle Native land claims so the land freeze could be lifted and the pipeline built. The climate was right because minority rights were a national concern in the 1960s. The Native's desire for a settlement, combined with the oil industry's need for a pipeline and the state's need for revenue, assured that Congress would give the land claims priority consideration. Interior Secretary Hickel helped to win support for the legislation by advising President Nixon that he should support the Native claim for 40 million acres in addition a cash settlement of $900 million over ten years. Egan, who was familiar with Washington D.C. from his two years as a Alaska-Tennessee Plan senator as well as his participation in the 1964 earthquake hearings, lobbied in the Capitol for prompt settlement. The Alaska Native Land Claims Settlement Act eventually passed Congress on December 14, 1971 with the Natives receiving $962.5 million cash, $500 million of which would come from state oil royalties, in addition to selection rights to more than 40 million acres. Ten days later, Interior Secretary Morton, who succeeded Hickel, established a 100-foot-wide oil pipeline corridor from Prudhoe Bay to Valdez. Neither the Natives nor the state could select land within this corridor. Egan's boyhood friend, John Kelsey, who managed the Valdez Dock Company, had been instrumental in convincing the oil companies that Valdez should be the tidewater terminus of the proposed pipeline. Although the state already owned some of the land over which the pipeline would travel, eminent domain or purchase from a few private inholders would be required. Meanwhile environmental litigation replaced Native land claims to block construction of the pipeline.

In October 1971, Governor Egan summoned eight of the top oil company executives to a meeting in Juneau at which he announced his plan to have the state of Alaska finance and own the pipeline. Egan feared that, under private ownership, high tariffs would decrease the value on which the state's royalty and severance taxes would be calculated. Furthermore, Egan believed that public financing could reduce costs, speed construction, and increase the value of North Slope crude oil. Pipeline ownership hearings began in March 1972. After a week of testimony the state and the oil companies were far apart. Some of the legislators had their own plan which involved right-of-way leasing of the pipeline corridor and Egan's plan for pipeline ownership was defeated in the Senate on a 17 to 3 vote.

With state ownership of the pipeline a dead issue, Egan introduced a cents-per-barrel tax so the state could place a floor beneath its oil income. This new tax would be a minimum charge per barrel and would smooth out fluctuations in the price of oil. Egan also proposed a 20-mill property tax on all oil field machinery in the state but local governments objected until a revenue sharing plan could be devised.

In October 1973, Egan called a special session of the Legislature to consider the oil package that Attorney General John Havelock had negotiated with the oil companies. This oil package consisted of a 25-cents-per-barrel minimum tax, a 20-mill property tax on pipeline facilities with a local government sharing feature, amendments to do away with the right-of-way leasing concept, elimination of the tariff-setting authority of the new Alaska Pipeline Commission, a one-eighth-cent-per-barrel conservation tax, some increase in the 8 percent severance tax, a common-purchaser/common-carrier pipeline bill, and a provision for the pipeline- owning companies to purchase the Valdez terminal site. Although some legislators considered these provisions too easy on the oil industry, the package passed.

While Egan and the Alaska Legislature were debating the oil package in Juneau, Alaska's senators, Ted Stevens

Governor William A. Egan, in cap and gown, with Neva, Dennis, and daughter-in-law Linda after receiving an honorary degree from the University of Alaska in Fairbanks in May 1972. Egan, who never was able to attend college received honorary degrees from both University of Alaska and Alaska Methodist University.—Photo courtesy of Neva Egan.

and Mike Gravel were working on ways to get the Alaska Pipeline Authorization Bill passed in Congress. An impending national oil shortage made action on the pipeline a priority, but court challenges from environmental groups barred the way. With Senator Stevens support,

Washington Senator "Scoop" Jackson drew up a Trans-Alaska Pipeline Right-of-Way Authorization Act that blocked the filing of environmental lawsuits. Senator Gravel forced an early vote on the bill to the annoyance of his colleagues. The bill passed with Vice President Spiro Agnew casting the deciding vote and was signed by President Nixon on November 16, 1973. A few days later, Governor Egan signed the state legislative package into law. In January, Nixon and Egan jointly executed a state-federal agreement pledging cooperative surveillance of the pipeline.

Once these obstacles were removed, work on the pipeline began in earnest. Before Egan could plan for usage of the anticipated increased state revenue once the oil began to flow, he had to win another election in 1974. Walter J. Hickel was his anticipated Republican opponent. However, Hickel was narrowly defeated by former state Senator Jay Hammond in the open primary election, possibly because some Democrats had crossed over and voted for Hammond hoping to assure Egan of a less formidable opponent. Television had become a major campaign medium and Egan, never a brilliant public speaker, was self-conscious when confronted with the cameras. Hammond, a handsome, bearded bush pilot from a Bristol Bay fishing village, was articulate, with a puckish sense of humor and a penchant for composing doggerel verse. He appealed to a new generation of Alaskan voters, who were unaware of Egan's own adventuresome youth, as the epitome of a rugged Alaskan. The election was close. After several recounts Hammond won by 287 votes, which he referred to as his "underwhelming victory".

Egan moved to Anchorage, where he became a manager for the Electrical Trust Funds of Local 1547 of the International Brotherhood of Electrical Workers and the Electrical Contractors' Association. During his years in Anchorage, Egan joined his former opponent, Walter J. Hickel, in founding Commonwealth North, a local think tank for consideration of Alaska's political and economic issues. He lived to watch Alaska deal with a glut of money from the oil revenues, but continued to regret that the state of Alaska did not own the Trans-Alaska Pipeline. He also regretted the 1980 cancellation of the state income tax that he had fought hard to establish as a young legislator in 1949. After Egan's death in May 1984, a memorial service was held in the new Anchorage convention center, built with oil money and named, the Egan Center, in his honor.

Surviving delegates and staff of the constitutional con-vention gather to celebrate the 25th anniversary of Alaska statehood in Fairbanks on January 3, 1984. The towns listed are those where the delegates lived at the time of the constitutional convention in 1955. Front row, left to right, Herb Hilscher, Anchorage; Jack Hinckel, Kodiak; Dora M. Sweeney, Juneau; William A. Egan, Valdez; Helen Fis-cher, Anchorage; Yule Kilcher, Homer; Dorothy Awes Haaland, Anchorage; Ada B. Wien, Fairbanks; Katherine Nordale, Juneau. Back row, left to right, Eldor R. Lee, Pe-tersburg; George Lehleitner, Tennessee Plan advocate; George Sundberg, Juneau; Rev. Roland Armstrong, Ju-neau; Seaborn J. Buckalew, Jr., Anchorage; Barrie M. White, Anchorage; John B. Coghill, Nenana; John S. Hel-lenthal, Anchorage; Leslie Nerland, Fairbanks; Burke Ri-ley, Haines; George Cooper, Fairbanks; Secretary Thomas B. Stewart, Juneau; Victor Fischer, Anchorage; James P. Doogan, Fairbanks; Clerk Katie Alexander Hurley, Ju-neau; Peter L. Reader, Nome; Maynard D. Londborg, Unalakeet; James Hurley, Palmer. William Egan, a heavy smoker throughout his life was already suffering from lung cancer when this picture was taken.—Photo cour-tesy of Neva Egan.

SOURCES

Much of the information in this book has been gained through interviews with people who knew Bill Egan during the years before he became governor of Alaska and during the first year of his first term. I am indebted to several persons still living who have been generous with their recollections. John Kelsey and George Sullivan knew Egan as a youth in Valdez. Victor Fischer, Burke Riley, Katie Hurley and Thomas Stewart served with Egan during the constitutional convention. Senator Ted Stevens worked with Egan when he was in Washington D.C. as a Alaska-Tennessee Plan senator. John Rader, James Fitzgerald and James von der Heydt were appointed to positions in the administration or judiciary by Egan in the first year of his first term. Above all, I am indebted to Neva Egan who has talked with me on numerous occasions and has been supportive of my efforts.

Several valuable collections of interviews with people no longer living have also been helpful. Gerald Bowkett, a former Egan press secretary who is now retired in Arizona, provided transcriptions of his interviews with Truck Egan, Alice Horton, Jim Dieringer, Marie Whalen and others, assembled while writing "Egan of Valdez" for *Alaska Journal* in 1984. Shortly after Egan's death, the oral history project at University of Alaska in Fairbanks recorded tapes of interviews with Egan associates such as John Dimond and John Butrovich. Finally, the Claus Naske Collection at the Rasmuson Library of the University of Alaska Fairbanks contains transcriptions of the interviews that Naske had with Marie Dimond, Mary Lee Council, Margery Smith, Vide Bartlett, Hugh Wade, and Bill Egan during the preparation of Naske's biography of Bob Bartlett.

Several videotapes of Egan himself gave me some insight into his own assessment of his career. KAKM in Anchorage provided me with a copy of the taped interview with Anita McGrath that they produced shortly prior to Egan's death in 1984. The Rasmuson Library had a videotape of an interview with Egan made for the 25th anniversary of the constitutional convention.

Several published sources provided valuable information:

Bowkett, Gerald E. *Reaching for a Star*. Fairbanks: Epicenter Press, 1989.

Fischer, Victor *Alaska's Constitutional Convention*. Fairbanks: University of Alaska Press, 1975.

Naske, Claus, *A History of Alaska Statehood*. Fairbanks: University of Alaska Press, 1975.

Gruening, Ernest, *Many Battles*. New York: Liveright, 1973.

Letters between Egan and Bartlett are in the Bartlett Collection at the Rasmuson Library, University of Alaska Fairbanks.

Additional information about Egan's early life in Valdez and about his years in the Alaska Territorial House and Senate has been accumulated from newspaper accounts in the *Valdez Miner*, Juneau's *Daily Alaska Empire*, the *Anchorage Times*, and the *Fairbanks Daily News-Miner*.

INDEX

A

Note: **Bold** type indicates a photograph of the subject.

C

D